The Healing Journey
for
Binge Eating
Your Individualized Path to
Recovery

By Michelle Market, LPC, CEDS

The Healing Journey for Binge Eating is published by
Michelle Market, LPC, CEDS
First Edition, December 2013

ISBN-13: 978-0615936697

Printed in the United States of America

Disclaimer
The information in this manual is not intended to provide medical advice and is sold with the understanding that the author is not liable for the misconception or misuse of information provided. This workbook is meant to complement treatment with an eating disorder professional it is **not** intended to replace counseling, therapy or medical treatment. All matters regarding one's health requires medical supervision.

This workbook is dedicated to my family, my mentors, and my clients.

Introduction

We live in a society that spends billions of dollars on diets. The how-tos are plentiful, while the underlying issues are ignored—a pattern that keeps the diet industry thriving and the dieter in a perpetual cycle of failure. Throughout the pages of *The Healing Journey for Binge Eating,* you will gain insight into the barriers preventing you from forming a healthy relationship with food and your body. You will gain an in-depth awareness and understanding of your inner dialogue and how this impacts your relationship with food and sense of self. You will learn to recognize your individual patterns that perpetuate the destructive cycle of an unhealthy relationship with food and your body. You will be encouraged to identify self-defeating attitudes and beliefs about your body. You will be provided with tools to create new intentions and healthy rituals to replace old habits that no longer serve you in your life.

Overcoming binge eating takes time, persistence, and patience. The *Healing Journey* series was designed to provide you a step-by-step individualized path to your own personal recovery. This is not a quick-fix program; this is a lifestyle change. In the neuroscience field, there has been a lot of dialoguing about rewiring the brain. "Neurons that fire together wire together." What that means is that the more consistent you are with implementing a new way of thinking around food, the more likely you are to create permanent change. Therefore, it is important not to rush the process.

This workbook can be read in order, or you may skip around depending on what your needs are at the time. Each chapter will serve as a piece of the puzzle of creating a healthy relationship with food. Each chapter will provide you with specific practices to implement as well as an opportunity for self-reflection. Just like putting a puzzle together, there is no specific order in which to use this workbook. It is designed to help you create your individualized plan.

It would be ideal to set an intention each time you open up your workbook. Create an intention to let whatever comes up for you and do so without censoring. Think of this workbook as an opportunity to look within. You have the answers within you, but you must slow down enough to listen.

We are a quick-fix society. Each day we are inundated with hundreds of messages about how to go about losing weight. You have heard the messages "Lose weight in two weeks," "Walk it off," "Fit into your favorite dress by Labor Day." No wonder diets have a 95 percent failure rate. They set you up for failure and leave you feeling like you will never overcome your relationship with food. That food has the power over you, and that it is you that failed and not the diet. They couldn't be more wrong. If you were sick and your doctor told you that they have an antibiotic that has about a 5 percent success rate, would you take it?

Probably not. Yet many keep getting back on the diet bandwagon time and time again.

I have a few requests for you as you embark on this journey: For the time being, please put weight loss on the back burner. I promise you will get to that, but if you make that the primary priority then you are just replicating another diet. As you begin reading this workbook you may find that your eating feels even more out of control. Please don't run for the hills. This is your bingeing asking you, *Are you really sure you want to give me up? Are you really sure you are ready? Do you really think you can do this?* Your bingeing might tell you, *I do such a great job of numbing you from your pain, from keeping you disconnected from your body, and from keeping you from getting hurt.*

The use of journaling is a helpful tool to connect with your feelings. By using the written word, you are slowing down your mind, giving you the chance to draw parallels between what is going on (events/triggers) and what your needs (emotions/feelings) are at that time. Throughout this workbook there will be many opportunities to journal. It is also helpful to have a separate journal to elaborate on questions that resonate and hit home. This will give you the chance to create a deeper understanding of why you have stayed connected to your relationship with food. Try not to censor your responses; those are your truths for right now. It takes a lot of courage to put those words on paper and connect to them.

I am here to help you start to disconnect from your relationship with bingeing and to start to connect with yourself. It is my wish for you that you will treat yourself with self-compassion and self-acceptance through this journey, thus allowing you to gain greater insight into this struggle. I look forward to being part of your recovery journey. In the words of Confucius, "A journey of a thousand miles begins with a single step."

In gratitude,
Michelle Market, M.Ed., LPC, CEDS

Table of Contents

Part One
Understanding Your
Relationship with Food

Notes:

Chapter 1
Creating Awareness

The first step in changing your relationship with food is becoming aware of the role of food in your life. Begin by taking an honest look at how you use food. Do you eat when you are sad, angry, bored, lonely, or any number of emotions that perhaps you are trying to avoid? Or do you eat when you are happy? Create awareness without being judgmental of the way that you use food. When you turn to food as comfort, most often it is in reaction to something. As you begin to check in with yourself and start to listen to your body and emotions, you will be given a window within to understand what is going on.

We all need a starting place; if you are abandoning dieting you have probably experienced many starts and stops in this process. I promise this time it will be different. Change is not a linear process. In fact, change can be very messy. It will look different for each person embarking on this journey. Each time you face an obstacle in your relationship with food, take a step back and look at the big picture. Use these obstacles as invitations to explore the underlying reasons that drive you to use food for coping, numbing, solace, or any number of reasons.

Take a moment and imagine a relationship with food where you are using food as nourishment, not for coping. You are eating when you are hungry, stopping when you are full. You are planning your meals instead of making choices based on your environment. You are honoring your needs. You are listening to your body. It is possible, it just requires patience. It is not about willpower, it is about believing in yourself. Healing is an inside job and you have the resources within you.

This journey that you are about to embark on does not have a timeline—it is individual for each person. The only comparison that should be done is with yourself. I was recently in a yoga class and had the instructor tell us to "stay on our own yoga mat" as a reminder to not compare with what others are doing in their practice. *You* are the expert on you, and as you embrace this journey, you will be creating attunement with your body. As you start to listen to your body and listen to hunger cues, you will create an awareness of what your body needs. Diets don't allow you to do that. In fact, diets move us away from learning to listen to our bodies. Diets are externally focused. When you are on a diet, something else (the plan, the diet flavor of the month) is telling you when and how much to eat. Attunement is internally focused. Being attuned with your body is being able to listen to your body and ask yourself what you are hungry for? Diets don't work because they are unrealistic and they create a sense of deprivation. When we tell ourselves something is off-limits, that often becomes the thing that we want. Take children, for example: Place them in a room with all their favorite toys, dolls, stuffed animals, and crafts, for girls; building blocks, trucks, and sports gear, for boys. Then tell them not to play with the remote-control car in the corner. When you leave the room, what do you think is the first thing that they want to play with? When you go on a diet and tell yourself you can't have ice cream, what is often the first thing that you crave? Your healing journey with binge eating will not be filled with comments such as:

"I want to lose twenty pounds in time for my sister's wedding next month."
"I will only eat salads for lunch and dinner."
"I will never eat sweets again!"

Begin to be very curious about the language that you use with yourself with respect to food choices. Food is not bad; it does not define whether we are a morally just person. However, when we label foods as good or bad we tend to judge ourselves as if we have committed a crime. When we truly listen to our body and ask ourselves what we are hungry for, we are practicing attunement.

What obstacles have gotten in the way of creating a healthy relationship with food?

_____

_____

_____

In what ways do you presently listen to your body?

_____

_____

_____

What role does food play in your life? Take the following self-assessment to help explore your present obstacles with food.

- ❑ I think about food all the time.
- ❑ After looking through fashion magazines, I feel worse about myself.
- ❑ I have dieted most of my life.
- ❑ I believe I will be happier when I lose weight.
- ❑ When I am on a diet, there are many foods I won't eat because I consider them "bad" or "forbidden" foods.
- ❑ I eat beyond fullness.
- ❑ I use food to cope with my feelings.
- ❑ I don't feel good about myself.
- ❑ I feel my eating is out of control.
- ❑ I hide my eating from others.
- ❑ I feel ashamed of my eating.
- ❑ I am concerned with what others think of me.

Reasons for Eating

When you use food as a distraction to deal with the feelings you are experiencing, you never learn to deal with the emotions directly. Food serves as a temporary distraction to avoid uncomfortable emotions. But what happens after the binge? You feel bad about yourself and you never actually dealt with what was truly going on. You end up still needing to deal with the original emotions *plus* the negative emotions that come up from overeating. Breaking the cycle of using food to cope with emotions is a slow and steady process. Throughout this workbook I will reference this cycle.

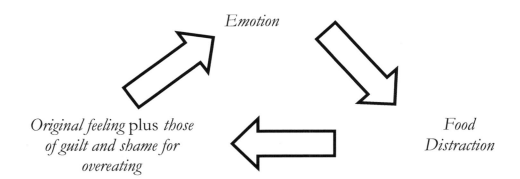

Anne, a thirty-three-year-old single woman, was feeling lonely being in her apartment by herself. Her relationship with food resulted in her isolating herself from others. She kept telling herself, *I will make plans with others when I lose weight.* But isolating from others actually resulted in her feeling lonelier. When Anne was feeling lonely, she would use food to numb herself from how she was feeling. After a binge, she felt upset with herself and experienced shame about using food to deal with how she was feeling. She wasn't dealing with feeling lonely or looking for ways to connect with others. Food did not address her loneliness. So after a binge she was still lonely, and she even felt worse about herself. The temporary distraction was only *temporary*!

As she worked on her healing journey, she got to a place where when she was feeling lonely she would call a friend, go outside, or play with her dog. She was yearning for connection, and food was not able to give that to her. As she began to break the cycle of using food to cope with loneliness, she found herself not feeling as pulled to food to deal with that emotion. This did not happen the first two or three times. This was something she spent about six months working on. She didn't put her life on hold until she lost weight or felt better about herself. Instead, she trusted the process and interrupted her pattern.

Remember when you first learned to ride a bicycle? At first it was awkward and uncomfortable, but then you got to the point where it became second nature. You may have been the type of child who got back on over and over again until you got it right. Or you may have been the child whose bike stayed in the garage because you were too afraid of getting hurt. Then, one day, you decided this was going to be the day to tackle this. It is important to honor wherever you are in the journey. If you spent a great deal of your life avoiding or being detached from your feelings, be patient as you learn to recognize those emotions that are coming up for you.

When we use food to cope with our emotions, it always deceives us. What is food replacing in your life? Are you avoiding dealing with disappointment or sadness? Are you in a difficult relationship? Are you unhappy or anxious about life?

_____

_____

_____

What feelings are you most afraid of?

_____

_____

_____

How Did Your Relationship with Food Begin?

Growing up, you learned certain things about the role of food. These messages might have been overt (out in the open) or covert (hidden and implied). In some families food is viewed as love, and all gatherings revolve around food. This would include my New York Italian family. A typical Thanksgiving is all your traditional fixings: turkey, mashed potatoes, green-bean casserole . . . you get the idea. But because food is love, my grandmother would bring a lasagna, and my aunt would make a ham. Don't get me started on the dessert and appetizer table!

Were you expected to eat everything on your plate? If you had a bad day at school, were you cheered up with a sweet treat? Were you told that you needed to eat all your vegetables in order to have dessert? Were you lectured about starving children and told not to waste any food? It is amazing to think of all the different connections we have with food, and how these relationships were molded at a young age.

What were the messages that you received regarding food in your household? How was dieting viewed in your family? Were foods categorized as good or bad?

_____

_____

_____

If you are a parent of small children, you have the opportunity to give them the gift of a healthy relationship with food. By being aware of your own food rules and how they have negatively impacted your relationship with food, you can serve as a positive role model for your children as they develop their own relationship with food.

What rules do you have about food as an adult?

_____

_____

_____

Describe your current relationship with food. In what areas do you want to improve? Describe what is going well in your relationship with food.

_____

_____

_____

The Process of Change

Look at where you currently are in your life. Is it realistic and reasonable to begin this journey? Do you tend to try to change everything at once? If the idea of beginning this journey feels overwhelming, then I encourage you to focus on one practice at a time. Why not begin with practicing self-compassion.

_____

_____

_____

How do you know if you are ready? This is a challenging journey and it is extremely important that you begin at a time in your life when you are ready. Of course, there is no perfect time. However, in order to set yourself up for success, be cognizant of your readiness to change. The five stages of change are problem recognition, concern, intention to change, optimism about change, and change. Notice which stage you identify with at this time.

Stage of Change	*Typical Response*
Problem Recognition – You are beginning to notice that your weight or how you use food is starting to become a problem.	o "I'm embarrassed about my weight." o "Since I have gained weight, I feel awful about myself." o "My eating is out of control"
Concern – At this point, you are concerned that your weight is impacting how you feel about yourself.	o "I can't keep up with my children." o "I'm tired of hiding behind my clothes. o "I feel terrible about myself."
Intention to Change – You are beginning to think about what you might do to address your concern.	o "I really want to do something about my eating." o "My schedule is so full that I am having trouble finding time to exercise."
Optimism About Change – You are feeling more enthusiastic about taking steps toward addressing your concern.	o "When I have nourished my body with a variety of foods, I felt great." o "When I have stuck to a consistent exercise plan, I've had more energy"
Change – You are taking the necessary steps toward a lifestyle change.	o "I am starting small and working toward improving my habits."

Which stage of change are you presently in? Are you ready to make this a priority?

_____

_____

_____

Sample Diet and Weight History

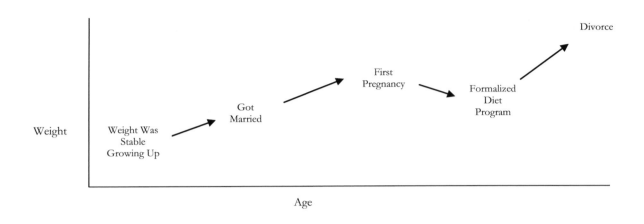

What patterns do you notice about weight gain with respect to milestones and/or life stressors?

_____

_____

_____

Describe your previous attempts to tackle your relationship with food.

_____

_____

_____

Do you have the support of others in this journey (i.e. friends and family)?

_____

_____

_____

How might others sabotage your efforts? How might you sabotage your efforts?

_____

_____

_____

Change is not an easy process. The following exercise demonstrates that. Take out a pen and paper and sign your name. Now switch hands and sign your name again. If you were to compare the exercise between both hands, what words would you use to describe each experience?

Dominant Hand (didn't have to think about it, comfortable, natural)

_____

_____

_____

Nondominant Hand (had to think about it, deliberate, it took longer)

_____

_____

_____

When you are changing your relationship with food and creating a new, healthier lifestyle, the change you experience will feel more like that of the nondominant hand. Eventually, as you start to retrain your brain and your body, it will get easier. Please don't be too quick to throw in the towel. Change is often made by taking a few steps forward and a few steps back. Soon enough, you will have fewer setbacks. Be patient in this journey. Remember, you are learning new skills that are going to impact the rest of your life. You did not learn unhealthy habits over night; the same holds true for developing healthy habits.

Together, we can work to take your relationship with food to the next level. Unlike the alcoholic, we can't abstain from food. Food is everywhere: celebrations, office parties, holidays, family gatherings, in vending machines, fast-food restaurants, food courts at the mall. To some extent, we are all emotional eaters, however when it starts to impact your happiness, when you are incessantly focused on food, and when it is interfering with your health, it is problematic. We need to learn a new way of using food in our lives. Food should be nourishment; food is fuel.

What is your current motivation to begin this program on a scale of 1‒-10? (10=highly motivated and 1=not ready at all)

_____

_____

_____

Why do you want to change your relationship with food?

_____

_____

_____

Is your motivation internally rooted (I am doing this for me) or externally rooted (I am doing this for my spouse, or because my doctor told me I need to do this)? Please explain.

_____

_____

_____

What is your attitude toward changing your relationship with food? (I am enthusiastic, I am moving forward with extreme skepticism)

_____

_____

_____

Do you have the time to commit to making these lifestyle changes? If not, how could you make the time?

_____

_____

_____

What is your vision for a healthy relationship with food?

_____

_____

_____

How do you imagine things working out if you do not change your relationship with food?

_____

_____

_____

What would be the best outcome if you were to embrace a program to tackle your relationship with food?

_____

_____

_____

If you were successful in healing from binge eating, how would your day-to-day life be different?

_____

_____

_____

How does bingeing impact your life?

_____

_____

_____

Physically?

_____

_____

_____

Emotionally?

_____

_____

_____

Financially?

_____

_____

_____

How does bingeing keep you from enjoying life?

_____

_____

_____

A routine question that I often ask a client when they come in for their first session is "If it weren't about food that you were coming to see me, then what would we really be working on?" Nine out of ten clients are stumped. But, after careful reflection and a few sessions under their belt, they start to share some of these underlying struggles such as perfectionism, fear of change, feeling directionless, unhappy in their current relationship, etc.

Conquering your food relationship begins with giving yourself permission to look at what feelings you might be avoiding and how you might be using food behaviors as a way to cope and or distract yourself from the real stuff.

Self-Compassion

Self-compassion is at the core of healing your relationship with food. How would you talk to your best friend, who is struggling with her relationship with food? How might you speak to a child? I suspect it would be with kindness, patience, and support. Why are you any different? You deserve to treat yourself with the same respect. Tough love and being hard on yourself will not motivate you to heal; if anything it might perpetuate the cycle. Over the years, I have noticed that those who are most successful with healing from binge eating have been able to soften the way they speak to themselves. It is time to distance yourself and disconnect from that critical voice in your head.

How are you practicing self-compassion in your life? In what areas of your life are you patient with yourself? What would be a small step toward practicing self-compassion in your day?

_____

_____

_____

Chapter 1 Summary
Creating Awareness

The first step in changing your relationship with food is becoming aware of the role of food in your life. Begin by taking an honest look at how you use food. Do you eat when you are sad, angry, bored, lonely, or any number of emotions that perhaps you are trying to avoid?

Reasons for Eating
When you use food as a distraction to deal with the feelings you are experiencing, you never learn to deal with the emotions directly. Food serves as a temporary distraction to avoid uncomfortable emotions.

How Did Your Relationship with Food Begin?
Growing up, you learned certain things about the role of food. These messages might have been overt (out in the open) or covert (hidden and implied). In some families food is viewed as love, and all gatherings revolve around food.

Self-Compassion
Self-compassion is at the core of healing your relationship with food. How would you talk to your best friend, who is struggling with her relationship with food? I suspect it would be with kindness, patience, and support. Why are you any different? You deserve to treat yourself with the same respect.

Self Reflection
What are my motivators for change? Am I ready to make my healing journey a priority?

Healing Practice
Be aware of your present relationship with food. Notice without judgment.

Notes:

Chapter 2
What Gets in the Way?

Healing gives you a voice, bingeing silences you.
Healing lets you find yourself, bingeing traps you.
Healing gives you an opportunity for growth, bingeing stunts any movement.
Healing gives you the opportunity to feel your feelings, bingeing numbs you.
Healing frees you, bingeing imprisons you.

Short-term discomfort is necessary in order to achieve long-term gain. In the summer, I am notorious among my family for being the last one to jump into the pool. I stick my toe in, I quickly pull it out. My kids yell for me to jump in on the count of three, they have to keep on counting. This goes on for at least an agonizing 10−15 minutes. Intellectually, I know that once I jump in it will take only a few minutes to get used to the temperature of the water. Physically, I resist. Emotionally, I know that once I get in I will have fun. But still I continue to experience this battle each and every time.

Recovery presents itself like this as well. There is short-term discomfort. The longer you avoid dealing with emotions and feelings, the harder it gets. The discomfort you experience will be the same whether you jump right into the pool or agonize over whether to jump in or not. But once you start the jump in it will get easier. You may have to practice recovery self-talk—*I can do this, I want recovery, I am worth it*—more abundantly in the beginning, and it may go on like that for some time. But the good news is that it is through our experiences of stretching out of our comfort zones that we truly grow.

I choose healing because I want freedom!
I choose healing because I want to live!
I choose healing because I am ready to fight!
I choose healing because I matter and I am worth it!
I choose healing because I want my life back!
I choose healing because I deserve it!

Identify your top five reasons for healing.

_____

_____

_____

_____

_____

_____

In what ways do you support yourself in recovery? Support can be defined as asking for help, being patient with yourself, or talking to yourself in a kind and loving manner.

_____

_____

_____

Now, let's take a look at sabotage. In what ways do you sabotage your own efforts toward recovery? Do you quit before you even start? Do you look for reasons why you will not succeed? Do you not make recovery a priority? Do you keep doing the same thing but expect different results?

_____

_____

_____

How might others sabotage your efforts of recovery? (i.e., Every time I begin to eat healthy, my sister invites me out for ice cream.)

_____

_____

_____

Sabotaging Statements

I don't believe I can.
I can't do this.
I can't allow myself to do this.
I have never been able, so what is different this time?
I don't have the time.
It won't put a dent in things.
What difference does it make?
It is a hassle.
It is uncomfortable.
This is too frivolous.
If eat something that wasn't healthy, then I am not going to be able to work that off.
My little walk is nothing in comparison to what I see others doing at the gym.
What is the point?
Nothing is going to be different.
Why bother?
This is too hard.
I can't succeed.
I'll never make peace with food.
I can't trust myself with food.
Food is the only thing that comforts me.
I'll never be happy with my body.
I don't deserve to take care of myself.

Identify the sabotaging thoughts that are getting in your way of having a healthy relationship with food.

_____

_____

_____

Turn Sabotaging Statements into Supportive Statements

Sabotaging Statement	*Supportive Statement*
I don't believe I can	I can do anything that I put my mind to. I am taking the steps to begin to heal my relationship with food.
I can't do this	I will keep putting one foot in front of the other.

I can't allow myself to do this	I deserve to heal my relationship with food.
I have never been able, so what is different this time?	I am cultivating a new understanding of what is keeping me stuck. I refuse to look at this healing journey as a diet with a timeline. I recognize that this is a process.
I don't have the time	I will make the time to make this a priority. I am recognizing my needs and my feelings and taking the time to honor both of them.

Shifting our beliefs means challenging old beliefs. It is sitting with new feelings and new thoughts which translate into a new way of being. Other examples of Supportive Statements to counteract self sabotage:

Every little bit does help.
If I stick with it, it will make a difference.
As I continue this journey, I do feel better.
It is temporarily uncomfortable as I begin, but as I continue at this, it will get easier.
I am worth taking the time for myself.
I choose to move my body to help my breathing, help my stress level,
and enhance the quality of my life.
I am not in a competition with anyone else.
I will not compare myself to others.
It doesn't have to be all or nothing.
I am approaching this in a new way that encourages me to delve into my underlying feelings
and to practice self-compassion.
I am learning to heal, and this process takes time.
I am learning to trust myself with food and to understand what my triggers are.
I am learning to do other things to comfort myself instead of turning to food.
I am beginning to accept my body.
I am doing the best that I can.
I am learning about the underlying pieces that maintain my present relationship with food.
I recognize that lifestyle changes do take a lot of work initially,
and I am being patient in the process.
By taking care of myself, I am showing myself and others that I am important.
I am learning to understand that the process of change takes time, and with every step I take,
I am working toward healing my relationship with food.

Identify the supportive statements that you can tell yourself about cultivating a healthy food relationship (i.e., One meal at a time, I am worth the time and investment, Progress not perfection). Take your sabotaging statements and turn them into supportive statements.

_____

_____

_____

What obstacles are getting in the way of you embracing recovery?

_____

_____

_____

What is the first small step you can take toward recovery?

_____

_____

_____

Cost-Benefit Analysis

What are the pros of Binge Eating?	*What are the cons of Binge Eating?*

What is your greatest fear about leaving bingeing behind?

_____

_____

_____

What has bingeing taught you?

_____

_____

_____

What does bingeing help you to avoid?

_____

_____

_____

Describe the anger inside you surrounding bingeing.

_____

_____

_____

Draw a picture relaying how you feel imprisoned by bingeing.

How has food been your friend?

_____

_____

_____

If you did not have bingeing, what else would you be focused on?

_____

_____

_____

Create Intention

The hardest part of treatment, by far, is following through with practicing skills between sessions or between groups. It is easy to be present in session and to brainstorm ways that things will be different when you leave the therapist's office. However, when you step onto the curb and into your car to drive back home, those intentions often fly out the window.

To make things a little simpler, I like to suggest that my clients set an intention each day, especially in the morning. What will you do today to support your relationship with food? Will you pack a lunch and healthy snacks? Will you take a break from your desk to eat uninterrupted? Will you go out for a walk when you hit that mid-afternoon slump that often sends folks running to the vending machine? What specifically will you do to take charge of your recovery?

I view creating an intention as building your own road map. Would you drive across the country without a road map? Of course you wouldn't. You would have an idea of what your destination is, the things you would like to see and do, a time frame, and a definite sense of direction. Why should creating a healthy food relationship be any different? Yet we often begin this journey of recovery without an intention, just desiring symptom relief. We want to get rid of bingeing. In the words of Vince Lombardi, "The quality of a person's life is in direct proportion to their commitment to excellence, regardless of their chosen field of endeavor." Intentions allow us to create a road map for recovery.

What are you willing to do to embrace recovery?

_____

_____

_____

What are you willing to commit to right now?

_____

_____

_____

What are you not *willing to do to embrace recovery?*

_____

_____

_____

When you begin the process of change, don't worry about doing it perfectly. Just getting started creates the necessary momentum. Each day is a fresh start. Do something small each day toward recovery. Every little step counts.

The other day I was brushing my six-year-old daughter's hair and had an epiphany. I recognized a parallel between recovery and keeping my daughter's hair tangle-free. When I brush it for a few minutes in the morning and at night, those knots stay away. But as soon as I skip a day (a common occurrence in my home), the knots get more and more complex. One day turns into two or three days, which then turns into an enormous bird's nest. I then feel overwhelmed and somewhat resentful for having to deal with this. The same pattern occurs: I am upset with myself for not paying more attention, I have to spend at least forty-five minutes gingerly working through the knots, and I beat myself up about the what-ifs.

Recovery is like this: You start by realizing that if you pack your lunch the night before and you start your day with a healthy breakfast, things run smoothly. You recognize that if you squeeze in some form of daily physical activity, you build momentum and enthusiasm for taking care of yourself. Creating a healthy lifestyle and a healthy relationship with food is something that must be done on a daily basis, not on a once-a-week basis. Cultivating these new habits takes time and initially may feel unnatural. However, as you continue to practice these skills, taking care of yourself will become as natural as brushing your teeth—you won't even have to think about it.

I am getting a lot better about tending to my daughter's hair on a daily basis, although there are days that I skip brushing it, throw her hair in a ponytail, and tell myself I will get to it tomorrow. It is a learning process, with many trials and errors.

What can you do to truly honor your needs and take care of yourself? Chances are you would be willing to do this for a best friend; why not do it for yourself?

_____

_____

_____

A word of caution: Please remember that life does not always go according to plan. Even the best-laid intentions can take a turn. But think of setting an intention as creating a guideline rather than a hard-and-fast rule.

Renew your commitment to yourself and to creating a healthy, balanced life. Start by creating your intention, and start simply. Create a vision for what you would like. Do you desire a healthy food relationship? Then define what that would look like, what it would feel like. Keep this written on an index card to serve as a reminder. Next, begin taking steps to make that intention become a reality. Remember, every little step counts.

For example, *today I will focus on noticing and honoring my hunger cues.* Or, *I will be prepared by having gone to the grocery store so that I will have healthy choices to choose from when I get home.* Start one step at a time, one intention at a time.

Today I commit to . . .
1. Starting my day with breakfast.
2. Moving my body on most days.
3. Eating a variety of foods.
4. Paying attention to hunger cues.
5. Eating without distractions.
6. Eating what I desire in moderation.
7. Increasing my fiber intake.
8. Bringing my lunch to work.
9. Getting eight hours of sleep per night.
10. Planning out my meals each week.
11. Packing healthy snacks when I am on the go.
12. Keeping a food journal to keep track of what and how much I am eating.
13. Understanding why I am eating at any time. Am I bored, tired, sad, or hungry?
14. Eating every 3–5 hours.
15. Practicing conscious eating.
16. Sitting down while eating.
17. Not eating in the car.
18. Having a designated eating spot in the house.

19. Grocery shopping from a list.
20. Not grocery shopping when hungry.
21. Abandoning the idea of diets. I will think in terms of a lifestyle change. I'll ask myself, *is this something I can do for the rest of my life?*

You can use the principle of intention with respect to planning meals and snacks or even more generally in your food relationship. Weekly intentions might take the form of incorporating healthy snacks, packing your lunch before work, or having meals planned throughout the week. Daily intentions look at what you will focus on that day. For example, sitting down while eating, eating in a designated eating spot, or noticing the taste and texture of what you are eating. The beauty is that you can to choose each day based on what is going on for you and where you need the most support that day. The reality is that those who are most successful are the ones who realize they are worth taking those extra ten minutes per day to pack their lunch or plan their meals. Becky timed how long it took to create a healthy salad to pack in her lunch bag. To her surprise, creating and packing this salad took only three minutes. Sometimes we perceive that things will take longer than they actually will. But she knew that taking those few minutes was important, because if she did not have that packed lunch, then she would have been more tempted to dine out with colleagues, which at the time was a very slippery slope for her. She knew that she was worth the extra few minutes that it took.

How might you incorporate intention with your food relationship? Resist the urge to try and do more than one thing at a time. When you are able to plan and have healthy food options readily available, you set yourself up for success. What intention can you create today to get you started?

_____

_____

_____

Choose an item in each category each day, to nourish your mind, body, and spirit.

Mind	Body	Spirit
☐ Reading	☐ Consistent meals	☐ Meditation
☐ Writing	☐ Movement	☐ Prayer
☐ Positive affirmations	☐ Connecting with others	☐ Having fun
☐ Focusing on other things	☐ Being grateful for your body	☐ Reaching out to a friend (having coffee with a friend)
☐ Watching a favorite TV show	☐ Conscious eating	☐ Laughing
☐ Learn something new	☐ Eating without distractions	☐ Listening to music
☐ Practice mindfulness	☐ Deep breathing	☐ Singing
☐ Be in the moment	☐ Resting	☐ Reading inspirational writings
☐ Practice self-compassion	☐ Listening to your body	☐ Practicing gratitude
	☐ Stretching your body	☐ Connecting with nature

Monday _____

Tuesday _____

Wednesday _____

Thursday _____

Friday _____

Saturday _____

Sunday _____

Chapter 2 Summary
What Gets in the Way?

Short-term discomfort is necessary in order to achieve long-term gain. Recovery presents itself like this as well. There is short-term discomfort. The longer you avoid dealing with emotions and feelings, the harder it gets.

Create Intention

The hardest part of treatment, by far, is following through with practicing skills between sessions or between groups. To make things a little simpler, set an intention each day, especially in the morning. What will you do today to support your relationship with food? Will you pack a lunch and healthy snacks? Will you take a break from your desk to eat uninterrupted? Will you go out for a walk when you hit that mid-afternoon slump that often sends folks running to the vending machine? What specifically will you do to take charge of your recovery?

When you begin the process of change, don't worry about doing it perfectly. Just getting started creates the necessary momentum. Each day is a fresh start. Do something small each day toward recovery. Every little step counts.

Self Reflection
What are the obstacles that I place in my path that makes change challenging?

Healing Practice
Each day take time in the morning to choose an intention to focus on. At the end of each day, reflect on what went well and what challenges you faced.

Chapter 3
Eating Triggers and Patterns

By exploring your pattern of eating, you will begin to uncover what your relationship is with food. Begin to pay attention and to be curious as to what a typical day looks like. Put judgment and critique on the back burner, and instead take an honest inventory of how you use food in your life.

Think over the course of the day.

- *Do you eat breakfast? What do you typically have?*

- *Do you snack between meals?*

- *Is there a time of the day that you find yourself craving certain foods?*

- *What foods do you typically consume in the course of the day?*

- *What is the toughest time of the day for you? What is the easiest time of the day for you?*

- *What does your nighttime eating look like?*

- *Do you find that you follow a rigid eating plan Monday through Friday and then binge over the weekend?*

What are your current eating patterns?

_____

_____

_____

Eating Styles

Styles of Eating	Typical Scenario
All-or-Nothing Eater:	"When I am on my diet, I am restricting my calories significantly; when I am off my diet, my eating is out of control." Strategy: Abandon the idea of dieting, as it sets you up for a greater sense of deprivation. Instead focus on doing things in moderation—whether it is eating or exercise.
Unconscious Eater:	When clearing the dinner plates, I find myself putting leftovers into my mouth, not even aware of what I am doing. I find myself eating while multitasking. Strategy: Focus on being in the moment with your eating. Eat without distractions. Turn off the TV. Take a break at lunchtime. Enjoy the experience of eating.
Caretaker Eater:	"I am always taking care of everyone else's needs." Caretaker eaters typically struggle with taking care of their own needs, often turning to food for comfort. Strategy: Constant caretakers need to recognize that their needs are important, too.
Social Eater:	"If it is in front of me, I will eat it." Social eaters find themselves indulging in foods that someone brought into the office, even though they had a balanced breakfast that morning. This eater does not check in with hunger cues. Strategy: Pay attention to hunger cues. You can be social without eating. Focus on conversation instead of consumption of unnecessary calories.
People Pleaser Eater:	"They will be upset with me if I don't eat." People-pleaser eaters struggle with not wanting to let others down. The end result is that they are the one who is being let down instead. Strategy: Pay attention to what you want and what you need. Is it fair for others to make you feel bad if you don't eat when you are not hungry?

Which eating style do you identify with most and why?

_____

_____

_____

Eating Triggers

As you create awareness around your relationship with food, begin to be cognizant of the reasons that you might be eating when you are truly not hungry. Could it be that you had just seen a commercial for fast food and you are suddenly craving the image that you saw? Have you had a hard day and find you have a craving for your favorite comfort food? Two common triggers for eating are emotions (sad, lonely, angry, bored, etc.) and environmental factors (seeing an advertisement, walking through the food court at the mall, driving past a restaurant).

Emotional Triggers

An emotional trigger is a feeling that serves as a catalyst to overeat. It can be a positive or negative emotion. Do you find yourself falling into the same food traps? Are you finding yourself eating out of boredom, to ease anxiety, to combat loneliness, or because it is habit? Instead of being critical, be curious. The first step is to create awareness as to what emotions trigger eating. If you use food to distract yourself from how you are feeling, you never actually address your feelings. Feelings are neither good nor bad—view them as information. Our feelings allow us to understand what is happening on an emotional level.

I eat when I feel . . . (Check off those that apply to you.)
- ❑ Angry
- ❑ Anxious
- ❑ Bored
- ❑ Depressed
- ❑ Happy
- ❑ Frustrated
- ❑ Jealous
- ❑ Lonely
- ❑ Tired
- ❑ Stressed
- ❑ Unhappy
- ❑ Upset

What other emotions serve as triggers for you to overeat?

_____

_____

_____

How might understanding emotional triggers help you change your relationship with food?

_____

_____

_____

Ways to Combat Emotional Triggers

Too often there is a tendency to want to disconnect and numb ourselves from the feelings that we are experiencing. Imagine you were driving on the freeway and suddenly you took your foot off the gas pedal and just slowly stopped. When we eat to avoid how we are feeling, it is as if we are that car on the freeway. Sometimes in life, we need to put on our hazards or pull off to the side of the road to diagnose and assess what is truly going on. But we never want to just stop in the middle of the road. When we avoid how we are feeling, we get stuck. When we push feelings down and keep pushing them down, they will pop up. As you begin to get in touch with how and what you are feeling, keep your foot on the gas. Be with your feelings, don't flee from them.

What are you looking for from food?

_____

_____

_____

Why is it hard to honor your feelings and emotions?

_____

_____

_____

What needs are currently being unmet?

_____

_____

_____

What emotions are you continuing to stuff?

_____

_____

_____

When You Are Feeling:	*Instead of Using Food to Cope, Try Instead:*
Angry	Take a time out. Give yourself time for self-reflection. Explore what happened that made you feel angry.
Anxious	Write down your worries and counteract them. Ask yourself: What is the evidence to support these worries?
Bored	Start a new hobby. Consider one that uses your hands and is not conducive to snacking (i.e. knitting).
Depressed	Talk to a counselor or close friend.
Frustrated	Go for a walk to clear your mind.
Happy	Celebrate using a non-food reward, such as buying flowers or treating yourself to a movie.
Jealous	Use journaling to write down what you are feeling.
Lonely	Call a friend. Have a plan for the times when you are most likely to feel lonely. Enroll in a class that you are interested in.
Tired	Take a nap. Pay attention to what your body needs.
Stressed	Take a yoga class. Focus on your breath.
Unhappy	Create a list of ten things for which you are grateful.

Environmental Triggers

An environmental trigger is a place or situation that serves as a trigger for you to overeat. It is not emotionally driven but a cue that can trigger an urge to eat when you are not hungry. It can be hearing about food, seeing someone else eat, or driving past your favorite restaurant. There are a variety of external cues that can trigger eating. For example, eating may be triggered by:

- o Watching a favorite TV show
- o Socializing with friends
- o Walking past a bakery or ice-cream shop
- o Driving past a fast-food restaurant

The important lesson is learning which social or environmental cues seem to encourage eating when you are not hungry, and then modifying those cues. This is known as stimulus control. The more often two things are paired together, the stronger the connection between the two becomes until, eventually, one triggers the other. For example, after repeatedly eating ice cream while watching a favorite TV show, just seeing a commercial for the favorite show may trigger a craving for ice cream.

What things (i.e. watching a movie, a certain time of day, driving) do you typically pair with eating? (i.e. The most challenging time of the day is nighttime, after I have eaten dinner. I am not ready to go to sleep, but I have a lot of unstructured time. I tend to watch a lot of TV to de-stress, and when I watch my favorite shows I always have my favorite foods in front of me.)

_____

_____

_____

The most challenging time will be different for each person. For many it is nighttime, right after dinner. For others it is when they get home from work. For some it is the mid-afternoon slump they feel when they are at work. Be curious about the patterns you have noticed with respect to your eating. This is not a time to allow your inner critic to take over. Instead, give yourself the space to practice self-compassion. Learn to become an observer of your body and your feelings.

What preventative measures could you take? (i.e. I can have a guideline where I only eat at my kitchen table, and after I have had my dinner or my evening snack I can then spend some time watching my favorite shows to de-stress. I do not need to use food to relax.)

_____

_____

_____

When Sarah would come home from work, she would go straight to her pantry. It became a weekday ritual for her. She would eat her favorite binge foods while standing in front of the pantry. Her eating trigger was just seeing the pantry. To begin to challenge this ritual, she started with being more mindful of what she was eating. The first practice she began was to sit down while eating, so grazing in front of her pantry was no longer an option. This was not a connection that she was able to break in a few days. As she challenged this pattern of eating, she initially experienced discomfort. There was a part of her that truly liked the work-to-home transition ritual. In addition, she was usually pretty hungry when she walked through the door. There was part of her that used food as an emotional comfort to disconnect from the events of the day. As she was challenging this eating pattern, she would stand in front of the pantry but bring her binge foods to the table. After a few days of that, she felt silly and realized that it was not interrupting and challenging the pattern, but instead perpetuating the cycle, and she still had her favorite binge foods as part of her de-stressing ritual.

She learned that the transition ritual had to begin before she even left the office. Before leaving work, she started eating a satisfying snack so that she was not so hungry when she first walked in the door at home. She began a new home-from-work transition ritual. Because she was no longer ravenous when she walked in the door, she began to go straight to her room and change out of her clothes into something comfortable, to signify that she was now home. She would then light a candle in her kitchen, play soothing music in the background, and take a few deep breaths. This calming ritual became a new script for her. She then went into the evening taking the time to prepare her dinner. She would check in with her body to determine what she was hungry for. She had interrupted the pattern of eating mindlessly. By taking some deep breaths, she was slowing down and found that she was not as stressed. She entered into the evening being more mindful.

In order to break the cycle of eating mindlessly, we need to identify and disconnect the triggers which result in overeating. The strength of the trigger diminishes over time as the two events are uncoupled. For Christine, an environmental trigger is eating in the car. Therefore, in an effort to eliminate the trigger, she adopted a new guideline and made the car a food-free zone. Initially, when she was in the car she felt the urge to eat, and not eating was a challenge, but over time it got easier as she broke this connection. There were times that she was not able to adhere 100% to her no-eating-in-the-car rule, but in those instances she was very aware and was eating mindfully. Those times became exceptions instead of the norm for her.

The following situations may serve as environmental triggers for you to overeat. Which ones apply to you?

- ❑ Being in the kitchen
- ❑ Being in the car
- ❑ Seeing fast-food restaurants
- ❑ At your desk
- ❑ Being in front of the TV
- ❑ Being at buffets
- ❑ Being at the mall
- ❑ Restaurants
- ❑ Being at family gatherings
- ❑ Seeing vending machines

Is there a particular spot in the house where you overeat? Or a particular place where you overeat?

_____

_____

_____

Ways to Combat Environmental Triggers

If You Tend to Overeat in This Situation: *Try Instead . . .*

In the Kitchen   Be aware of your hot spots. Is it in the evening after dinner? If so, set a time that you will not go into the kitchen. (i.e. I will not go into the kitchen after 8 PM.) Have a designated eating spot in the kitchen where you sit down and eat.

In the Car   Because you are practicing conscious eating, have a guideline that your car will be a food-free zone.

Fast Food Restaurants   Go in with a plan. Know what you are going to order ahead of time. There is convenience in fast food, however there can also be traps. Stay in touch with what you are hungry for.

At Your Desk   It is very important to take a break during the day. Research indicates that you are more productive when you take a break than when you work through lunch. If you must stay at your desk, then turn off your computer and take twenty minutes to just focus on your lunch. Eat without distractions.

In Front of the TV   It is very easy to overeat in front of the TV simply because your focus is on the television and not what you are putting in your mouth. If you must eat in front of the TV, pay attention to portion sizes. Instead of eating out of the bag of pretzels, measure out a serving size and put the bag away. Or better yet, designate a spot in your home for eating (i.e. kitchen table or dining-room table).

At the Mall   Don't go shopping when you are hungry. Pack a healthy snack pack so you can pay attention to hunger cues. If in the beginning you find the allure of the food court too overpowering, don't go past the food court. Pay attention to your own traps. Don't try to willpower your way through this; Instead, if it is too tempting, do something different.

Buffets   The overabundance and accessibility of food can trigger feelings of wanting to get your money's worth. So many delicious options. To get your money's worth, load up on seafood that has been baked or broiled. Chose items that you would not normally have. Select only a few things as opposed to wanting to try everything.

At the Grocery Store	Sometimes seeing food in front of you serves as a trigger. At the grocery store, avoid checkout lines with a candy aisle. Ask yourself, "Do I want the chocolate bar because I am craving chocolate, or is because it is in front of me that I am buying it?"
Sit Down Restaurants	A typical restaurant portion size is three to four times larger than a recommended serving size. Do you have any beliefs about dining out? Do you believe that dining out makes the meal a special occasion? Be aware of hidden calories and various traps that you might fall into. Do you load up on the bread before your meal arrives? Do you order an appetizer, main entrée, and dessert? Choose an appetizer or a dessert with your main meal, instead of both. Split a dessert or an appetizer with a friend. When your entrée arrives, ask for a takeout container so that you can immediately take half of your meal and save it for lunch or dinner the next day. Pay attention to hunger and fullness during your meal.
Family Gatherings	Enjoy the social component of being with your family. Pay attention to how you are feeling. If food is love in your family and the choices are plentiful, then choose your favorite things that perhaps you can't get all the time.
Vending machines	Try instead to pack your own mid-afternoon snacks from home so to not fall into this slippery trap. If your only option is using the vending machine, then choose snacks that have protein in them (i.e. nuts)

Other Ways to Eliminate Environmental Cues

Have healthy foods easily accessible in your home. Keep cut vegetables on the top shelf of your refrigerator so they are the first thing you see when you open the door. Have a fruit basket sitting on your kitchen table.

Practice portion control. If chips or cookies set you up for a binge, only purchase single portion sizes. You may spend a little more money, but you will certainly save on calories.

Keep trigger foods out of sight. If you keep a bowl of candy on your desk, you will be more likely to eat when you are not hungry, simply because it is in front of you. Move the candy or the trigger food so that it is not in your direct line of vision.

Carry a healthy snack pack with you. This helps when you are running errands, eliminating the need to be tempted by environmental cues. Pay attention to hunger cues and what you are hungry for.

Self-Monitoring

An effective tool in your healing journey is the use of food journaling. A food journal enables you to become aware of everything that you put into your mouth. By monitoring and recording your food consumption, you are acknowledging each time you indulge. Therefore, you can break the cycle of unconscious eating. You are now giving yourself the opportunity to turn unconscious eating into conscious eating. You may be surprised by what you discover. A food journal is meant to collect data and information so that you can determine what traps you fall into.

Do food journals bring up thoughts and feelings about diets of the past? Instead, think of this tool as collecting data to help identify food triggers and look at eating patterns. They help to look at the spacing of meals (i.e. are you eating lunch at 11:00 and then not eating dinner until 7:00 and are wondering why you are feeling ravenous and why it sets you up for an all-out binge?). Are you eating mindlessly and not realizing what you are putting in your mouth because you are eating through lunch or while watching TV?

Does the thought of writing down everything you might eat while bingeing make you rethink what you chose to eat? Food journals can be very beneficial when used to address what is going on with your challenges in creating a healthy food relationship. If you feel overwhelmed with starting one, start by just recording what you eat during your most vulnerable time of the day. If you find your desire to binge is greatest between 6 PM and 10 PM, then use a food journal during those hours to capture what you are actually consuming. Don't judge it; instead use it as a way to create an understanding of what might be going on.

When making a behavior change and trying to take notice of eating patterns, the following components are essential for a comprehensive food journal.

What time of day is it?
   o   Begin to notice patterns. Are there certain times of the day when you eat more? How much time are you allotting between meals?

What type of meal?

- o Take note of whether this is a structured meal, a snack, or if you are grazing.

What did you eat, and how much?

- o Did you eat a serving size of ice cream (1/2 cup) or a bowlful of ice cream (up to 4 servings)?
- o Become cognizant of portion sizes.

What is your initial hunger level?

- o Are you eating because you have been prompted by hunger cues, or are you eating out of emotional hunger?
- o 1–4: eating out of physical hunger
- o 6–10: eating out of emotional hunger
- o If you eat at a 1 or 2 (ravenous), you will tend to overeat. When you are eating at below a 5, you are eating out of physical hunger. When you find yourself eating at a 6 or more, you might be eating for emotional reasons. Ask yourself what purpose food is serving you. The art of following hunger cues is a balancing act. It is not allowing yourself to get too hungry or too stuffed. Try eating at a 3 and stopping at a 5.

Hunger Scale
1. You are so hungry you feel light-headed and dizzy.
2. You need to eat, you feel irritable and cranky. You feel ravenous.
3. Your stomach is growling.
4. You're experiencing continued hunger signals.
5. You feel just right – neither hunger nor full.
6. You are comfortably full, a little full.
7. You feel very full.
8. You feel uncomfortably full.
9. Your stomach is so full that it hurts a little.
10. You've eaten so much you feel stuffed beyond capacity.

Where were you eating?

- o This creates greater awareness regarding the environmental situation. Are you sitting at your kitchen table being in the present moment with your food?

Were you doing anything else while eating?

- Are you eating with distractions, such as eating in front of the TV or while standing up? There is a tendency to overeat when you are multitasking while eating.
- Also, take into consideration how fast you were eating. Did it take you under five minutes to eat your meal? Remember, it takes the stomach about twenty minutes to recognize when it is full.

How are you feeling?

- Begin to make the connection between what you are eating, how much, and how you are feeling. Are you eating because you are hungry, sad, angry, or tired?

What is your ending fullness level?

- Are you finished eating when you are satiated, or are you eating beyond comfort?

When you begin to acknowledge that what you are putting in your body includes things such as licking the peanut butter off a knife, eating the two chicken nuggets your son didn't finish, snacking while you are preparing dinner, snacking while you are putting away the dinner dishes, reaching for a handful of M&M's at work, and indulging in office donuts after you had a balanced breakfast at home, the list becomes endless; There are many ways that unneeded calories sneak in.

Sara's Food Journal
Date: June 4th

Time	Type of Meal B/L/D/S (Breakfast, Lunch, Dinner, or Snack)	What did I eat and how much?	Initial Hunger Level (1–10)	Where was I eating (environment)? (kitchen, office, living room) Was I doing anything else while I was eating? (i.e. watching TV, standing up)	How am I feeling?	Ending Hunger Level (1–10)
7:00 AM	B	Bowl of cereal with milk; Coffee	2	Standing at the kitchen counter	Tired	5
10:00 AM	S	2 donuts	4	At the office. Someone brought in donuts for a meeting.	Stressed	6
2:00 PM	L	Ham-and-cheese sandwich with mayonnaise; Potato chips; Diet soda; 1	1	Office cafeteria. Sitting at a table.	Hungry	7
3:30 PM	S	Handful of candy	2	At the candy bowl in front of coworker's desk	Tired	4
6:15 PM	S	Handful of crackers; ½ candy bar	1	Ate while preparing dinner	Rushed	5
7:00 PM	D	Bowl of pasta; 3 pieces of bread with butter	2	Ate while sitting in front of the TV	Hungry	7
9:30 PM	S	Pint of gourmet ice cream	5	Ate in den while watching TV	Lonely	9

Take a look over Sara's food journal. What hidden traps do you notice in her day? What coping skills would you suggest to her?

_____

_____

_____

What Sara learned from this exercise is that much of her unplanned eating during the day was the result of food being made available by others in her office. She made the connection that at lunch and dinner she was waiting too long to eat and was ravenous when she sat down to eat her dinner, which resulted in overeating.

In Monica's case, her biggest complaint was the time it took to keep a food journal. So instead, since evenings were the most challenging time for her, she had a journal on her refrigerator to record her eating patterns at that time. She found that, on many occasions, this technique interrupted her emotional eating that occurred at night. It also made her aware of the difficulty she had with food when she had unstructured time. It forced her to think about ways she could add more balance in her life. She spent the hours between 8 AM and 5 PM at work, but had nothing going on in the evening. She decided to take a photography class through a local college. This gave her something to look forward to in the evening.

What ways does food sneak into your day? Take out a sheet of paper or use the blank food journal on page 165. What patterns do you notice?

_____

_____

_____

Behavior Chains

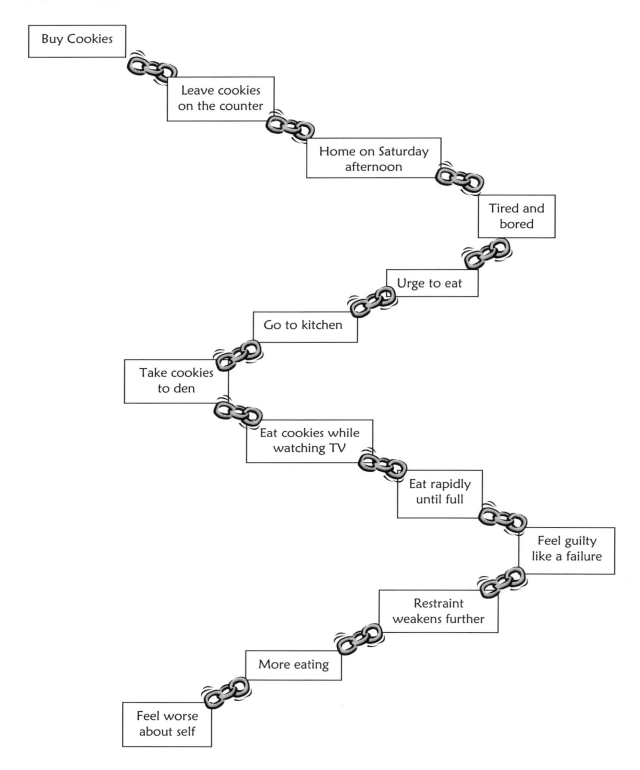

Buy Cookies

Leave cookies on the counter

Home on Saturday afternoon

Tired and bored

Urge to eat

Go to kitchen

Take cookies to den

Eat cookies while watching TV

Eat rapidly until full

Feel guilty like a failure

Restraint weakens further

More eating

Feel worse about self

If you look at the example presented, what seems to be a dietary lapse can be linked to a series of small decisions and behaviors. Behavior chains serve as a tool to intervene to prevent unwanted eating. Behavior chains involve looking at environmental cues as well as emotional cues that trigger overeating. When breaking a behavior chain associated with eating, the resulting strategy may be to sever the association of eating from the cue, avoid or eliminate the cue, or change the circumstances surrounding the cue.

Interrupting the Behavior Chain

Behavior	Alternative Behavior
Buy cookies	Knowing that cookies are a trigger food, don't bring them into the house, if this feels too overwhelming at this time in your recovery.
Leave cookies on the counter	Put away trigger foods. In general, visible food items are often cues for unplanned eating.
Tired and bored and feeling the urge to eat	Acknowledge your feelings. If you are tired, take a nap. If feeling bored, have an activity planned.
Take cookies to the den	Have designated eating spots in the house: the kitchen or dining room table
Eat cookies while watching TV	Eat without distractions. If you are feeling like eating some cookies, measure out a serving size. Enjoy every bite instead of eating rapidly until you are full.
Other ways to interrupt behavior chains	Slow the rate of eating to allow fullness signals to begin to develop before the end of the meal. Use smaller plates so that moderate portions do not appear to be meager.

Activity:

Create your own behavior chain. What ways might you interrupt the chain next time? Take notice of your environmental and emotional triggers

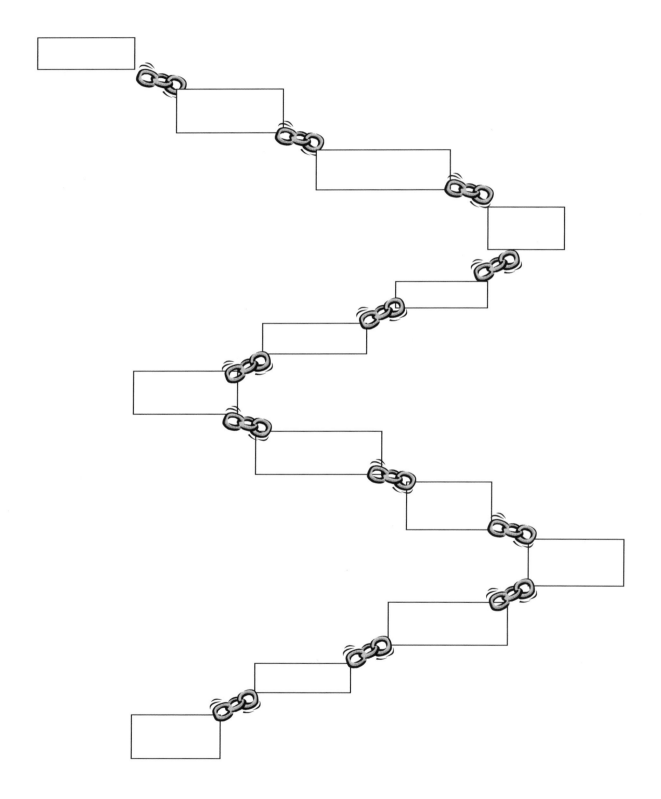

Chapter 3 Summary
Eating Triggers and Patterns

Emotional Triggers

An emotional trigger is a feeling that serves as a catalyst to overeat. It can be a positive or negative emotion.

Environmental Triggers

An environmental trigger is a place or situation that serves as a trigger for you to overeat. It is not emotionally driven but a cue that can trigger an urge to eat when you are not hungry.

Trigger Foods

Trigger foods are foods that once you start eating, you feel that you can't stop.

Self Reflection

What am I truly needing when I eat when I am not physically hungry?

Healing Practice

Over the course of the week take notice of when you are eating when you are not hungry. Record the emotional and environmental trigger. In addition, take note of your trigger foods.

Notes:

Chapter 4
How Are You Using Food to Cope?

When you use food as a distraction to deal with the feelings you are experiencing, you never learn to deal with the emotions directly. Food serves as a temporary distraction to avoid uncomfortable emotions. But what happens after the binge? You feel bad about yourself and it creates a vicious cycle of self-abuse. You end up still needing to deal with the original emotions and the negative emotions that come up from overeating. Breaking the cycle of using food to cope with emotions is a slow and steady process.

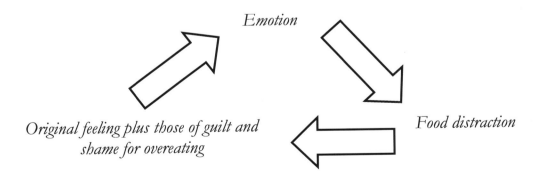

Emotion

Food distraction

Original feeling plus those of guilt and shame for overeating

Remember when you first learned to ride a bicycle? At first it was awkward and uncomfortable, but then you got to the point where it became second nature. If you spent a great deal of your life avoiding or being detached from your feelings, be patient as you learn to recognize those feelings that are coming up for you.

How Am I Feeling?

Check in with how you are feeling. Reflect over the past twenty-four hours. Is there an unresolved issue still on your mind? How are you feeling right now?

angry	*depressed*	*upset*	*irritated*	*stressed*	*fearful*
hurt	*lonely*	*anxious*	*at ease*	*fatigued*	*indifferent*

I am feeling _____*(emotion) because*

_____

_____

_____

Once you have identified your feeling, deal with it directly and appropriately. If you are tired, take a nap. If you are restless, find something interesting to do. If you are hungry, eat. Coping directly with emotions will at first feel difficult. You will need to concentrate on it, make it a priority. As you practice, it will be easier and begin to flow effortlessly. If you ate away any negative feelings, it can feel scary to acknowledge those feelings. You may have spent some time feeling ashamed of your feelings. Or perhaps you were taught not to make any waves, so you grew accustomed to stuffing your feelings.

What is the cost of eating to cope with my feelings? Will I feel worse if I choose to cope by eating?

_____

_____

_____

Are you using food as a distraction? Betsey had a fight with a coworker and felt angry. Her initial feeling was anger. Growing up, she never learned to deal with uncomfortable feelings, and instead would avoid those feelings, especially anger. After this incident with her coworker, she immediately went to the cafeteria at the office and overate, taking in unnecessary calories. She was using food as a distraction. However, the end result was that she became angry at herself for overeating, and she still felt angry about the incident with her coworker.

What Do I Choose to Do?

To break the cycle, acknowledge the feelings and use a behavior other than eating to deal with them. A non-food coping strategy can be an action, aside from eating, that results in helping you feel better. It is a healthy way to deal with uncomfortable emotions.

Unhealthy Coping Skill	*Healthy Coping Skill*
Excess shopping	Going for a walk
Binge eating	Watching an uplifting movie
Excess sleeping	Taking a bubble bath
Isolating	Calling a friend

When I have the urge to binge I can . . .

- o go for a meditative walk
- o sit near water
- o play calming music
- o drink my favorite tea
- o color in a coloring book
- o call a friend
- o write in my journal
- o watch a movie
- o join a support group for binge eating

Create your list of alternatives.

_____

_____

_____

Self-Care Box

A self-care box is a collection of your favorite things in one spot. Use it when you feel the urge to binge, or when you are upset, angry, bored, etc. Place it in a spot where you will see it. For example, if you tend to binge at nighttime, place it on your kitchen table.

Supplies needed: shoebox or a photo box, index cards, magazine clippings, and you can pick and choose the following items to place in the box

Take into consideration your five senses.

See: Buy a bouquet of flowers. Notice the spring flowers, the budding trees. Look at pictures that bring you a sense of calm (i.e. old vacation spots)

Hear: Call a friend. Listen to calming music. Sit near a stream and notice the sound of the running water.

Smell: Light a favorite scented candle. Rub scented hand lotion on your hands. Take a sliced apple, cinnamon sticks, and whole cloves; add two cups of water; and simmer on your stove.

Taste: Enjoy a cup of warm tea or hot chocolate. Mindfully eat your favorite piece of candy.

Touch: Wrap yourself in your favorite blanket. Take a bubble bath. Pet an animal. Play with clay.

The goal of trying these different self-soothing skills is to teach yourself how to calm and comfort without the use of food or the use of your eating disorder. Here are some other ideas to add into your coping box:

- o Favorite CD
- o Stationary
- o Aromatherapy candle
- o Bath salts or bubble bath
- o Chewing gum or mints
- o List of favorite websites (recovery-based)
- o DVD (comedy)
- o List of friends to call
- o Inspirational book or quotes
- o List of your top-five supports
- o Journal
- o Favorite affirmations
- o Silly putty
- o Magazines (that do not make you feel worse after reading them!)
- o Craft supplies
- o Postcards and photographs of places you have traveled or would like to visit

- o Create a list of things that you can do, such as: watch a sunset; listen to music; take a warm, relaxing bath; get a massage; practice yoga; mediate; breathe
- o Coloring book
- o Crayons, markers, and colored pencils
- o Bubbles
- o Lavender
- o Stress ball

Portable Coping Box (a version you can carry around with you):

- o Inspiration cards
- o Mint
- o Stones with powerful words (i.e. *growth, believe, transform*)
- o List of supports
- o Pictures of things that make you feel calm

Create a list of items you would place in your self-care box. Come up with at least five items.

_____

_____

_____

"When I'm hungry, I eat what I love. When I'm bored, I do something I love. When I'm lonely, I connect with someone I love. When I feel sad, I remember that I am loved."
—*Michelle May, M.D., Eat What You Love, Love What You Eat*

Imagine it is Thursday night and you've had a rough week at work: You are tired, you feel overwhelmed, and you are exhausted. Upon entering your home, knowing all these emotional triggers are active within you, you walk straight into the kitchen and open the pantry and begin grazing, not knowing what exactly your body wants or needs. This has been your Thursday ritual for as long as you can remember. You are numb to what is going on in your body. You are on autopilot. You are subconsciously protective of this pattern and find that by Thursday you are just too tired to be "good."

Now, I want you to imagine another scene. It is still Thursday night, and you are still feeling burnt out from your rough week at work. You are tired, overwhelmed, and exhausted. You hang up your jacket and walk into your kitchen.

This time you notice the bouquet of sunflowers that you had purchased for yourself earlier this week and some gourmet chocolates with uplifting messages in the wrappers. You notice the sign you made for yourself that states "What can I do to take care of myself today?" You sit down at the kitchen table and pour yourself a cold glass of water. You unwrap the beautiful gold foil and read the first message: "In life's winter, find your invincible summer." You allow yourself to taste the dark chocolate and slowly let it melt in your mouth. You reflect over your day and acknowledge that it has been a tough week and that you worked longer hours than usual. You unwrap a second chocolate to be met with the message that "Life is too short to waste." You think about what you need right now and remember that you had just purchased the newest book from your favorite author. You make the plan that after dinner you will draw a warm bubble bath and indulge in reading a few chapters of your new novel before turning in for the night.

Often our patterns keep us stuck doing the same thing each day. Start to imagine how you can rewrite the script. How might you do something different? What visual reminders would you need in order to create a new ritual? Is it a note? Is it your self-care box sitting inside of your pantry? Initially, taking a bubble bath and curling up with your favorite author will not feel the same as numbing out. It may even feel surprisingly painful, but I encourage you to push through the discomfort. Take it slow and steady. Buy yourself your favorite bouquet of flowers—you are worth it.

Chapter 4 Summary
How Are You Using
Food to Cope?

How Am I Feeling?
Check in with how you are feeling. Reflect over the past twenty-four hours. Is there an unresolved issue still on your mind?

angry	*depressed*	*upset*	*irritated*	*stressed*	*fearful*
hurt	*lonely*	*anxious*	*at ease*	*fatigued*	*indifferent*

When I have the urge to binge I can . . .

- o   go for a meditative walk
- o   sit near water
- o   play calming music
- o   drink my favorite tea
- o   color in a coloring book
- o   call a friend
- o   write in my journal
- o   watch a movie
- o   join a support group for binge-eating

Self Reflection
What is my fear with using non-food coping skills?

Healing Practice
Create urge cards that will serve as reminders of non-food coping skills to address your feelings. (*e.g. When I am sad I can call a friend, when I am angry I can go for a walk, when I am stressed I can breathe*).

Notes:

Part Two
Slowing Down

Chapter 5
Self-Care 101

Self-Care

- Do you feel cheated out of time for yourself?
- Has your favorite hobby been put on the back burner?
- Do you feel guilty when you take a vacation?
- Have you been putting off getting regular exercise?
- Do you skimp on sleep in an effort to get more things done in your day?
- Is your eating chaotic?
- Are you overcommitted in your schedule?

If you answered yes to any of these, it may be time to pay closer attention to self-care. If you have ever traveled on an airplane you have probably heard the flight attendant gently remind you to put on your own oxygen mask first in an emergency before assisting others. Similarly, in your personal life, if you do not first meet your own needs, it can be quite difficult to have the energy or resources to take care of others. An uncompromising regimen of self-care is in effect the daily dose of oxygen you need to store up your physical and mental resources. One common denominator among people who struggle with disordered eating is the lack of ability to practice self-care.

But what exactly is self-care? Sleep, good nutrition, and exercise are at the core of self-care. However, that's not where self-care ends! Self-care also entails nurturing yourself emotionally, physically, and spiritually. In order to accomplish this, it is vital to carve out time for yourself, to allow for rejuvenation. One caution: Sometimes, when we think we have to "take care of ourselves," we create rather elaborate plans that just don't get put into play. Rather than thinking on such a large scale, however, the key is to start small. Even simple pleasures can bring increased joy into your life.

Self-nurturance is difficult for many. Do you give yourself what you need? Do you sleep when you are tired? Do you eat when you are hungry? Do you enjoy your solitude when you need to be alone? Self-care does not have to be monumental; every little bit counts. A self-care plan is a specialized plan that you create to take care of yourself, especially during difficult times. The core of an effective self-care program includes adequate sleep, a healthy eating plan, regular exercise, relaxation, and creating and utilizing a support system. Taking care of yourself is a way to assist in managing your life and life stressors. It also impacts your relationship with food. When you are practicing self-care, chances are you are taking the time to have healthy foods available, you are slowing down enough to listen to what your body needs, and you are tending to your stress.

When you read the statement "treat yourself as a loving and kind friend," what emotions and reactions surface for you? How do you feel about the statement? Is this a truth that you live by?

_____

_____

_____

Why is it challenging to be supportive of yourself? What can you do to recognize that your needs are important?

_____

_____

_____

What are some needs that you have neglected? (i.e., Taking time for myself, Listening to my needs.)

_____

_____

_____

What gets in the way of you taking care of yourself? (i.e. guilt, not knowing how)

_____

_____

_____

What is something small you have done to take care of yourself today?

_____

_____

_____

What if instead of focusing only on food, we made a commitment to take care of ourselves differently? What that might look like is, "Wow, I am really tired. I could use a nap," instead of going to chocolate and/or coffee (fill in the _____) for the pick-me-up. Or acknowledging that "I am really sad that my friend passed away," and allowing yourself to feel instead of turning to food for comfort. It is about asking ourselves—tuning into your body instead of tuning out.

If you are juggling many balls at once (i.e. work assignments, family commitments, friends, volunteering, health) it can be easy to drop a ball. If you are too focused on meeting the needs of others, how on earth are you going to be able to meet your own needs?

How can you perform well in other areas of your life (i.e. work, relationships) if you are not taking care of yourself?

_____

_____

_____

Self-Care Needs Assessment

Use this assessment to track how things are going. Take note of any deficits and areas for improvement. Use the space below each category to describe what is getting in the way of practicing self-care in that area.

Physical (body):

- ☐ Do I get enough sleep each day?
- ☐ Do I move my body consistently? (i.e. walking, swimming, or some form of exercise I enjoy)
- ☐ Do I nourish my body at regular intervals throughout the day?
- ☐ Do I meet my nutritional needs on most days?
- ☐ Do I take time off of work when needed?
- ☐ Do I take time to breathe and slow down?

_____

_____

_____

Emotional (mind):

- ☐ Do I say affirmations?
- ☐ Do I write in a journal?
- ☐ Do I actively reduce stress in my life?
- ☐ Do I say no?
- ☐ Do I spend time with individuals who I enjoy being around?
- ☐ Do I participate in individual therapy or group support?

_____

_____

_____

Spiritual:

- ☐ Do I reach out to friends?
- ☐ Do I take time for quiet reflection each day? (i.e. prayer, meditation)
- ☐ Do I read inspirational writings?
- ☐ Do I spend time in nature and appreciate my surroundings?
- ☐ Do I know what is meaningful in my life?
- ☐ Do I know my values and passions in life?

_____

_____

_____

In what areas (i.e. body, mind, spirit) do you notice a deficit? What areas of your life are in balance?

_____

_____

_____

What is depleting you?

_____

_____

_____

What is energizing you?

_____

_____

_____

What do you need more of?

_____

_____

_____

What do you need less of?

_____

_____

_____

Here are a few ideas to get you thinking about your own self-care plan. Check off those that you would be willing to experiment with:

- o   Turn off your phone when you want some uninterrupted time.
- o   Listen to relaxing music at home.
- o   Plan fun and/or relaxing activities into your day on a regular basis.
- o   Focus on daily pleasures (i.e. the change of the leaves, the smell of cookies baking).
- o   Schedule a "me date"—blocking out time just for you on a weekly basis.
- o   Schedule physical activity into your day—just 10 minutes can give you a boost.

Pay attention to the times that you are able to nurture or soothe yourself, even if it is just a little bit. Make a note of when are you able to do this. What are you doing when you nurture yourself? Take notice of what is different about these times. How were you feeling? What were you thinking?

_____

_____

_____

What things must I start doing?

_____

_____

_____

What things must I stop doing?

_____

_____

_____

Incorporating Joy into Your Life

What brings you joy in your life? Are you open to allowing that joy in? Are you beginning to have an understanding of the way that you may hinder your own progress? As part of your healing journey, cultivate awareness around what brings you joy and satisfaction in your life (i.e. reading, traveling, writing). Is there a way to incorporate more joy in your life starting today? What things are you putting on the back burner until you lose weight, make peace with food, or get a handle on your food relationship? Start living your life today, instead of putting your life on hold.

In what ways have I put my life on hold?

_____

_____

_____

Often in life, there are many things out of our control. When we are feeling stressed or irritable, it is a sign that something has to change. If you are finding yourself using food to sooth, don't beat yourself up; turn off the inner critic and tap into your inner advocate. Change the inner dialogue in your head to be one of compassion. Self-care is synonymous with self-compassion. Ask yourself what you need. Commit to doing one thing every day that makes you feel good. Perhaps it is reading a few pages of your favorite author, watching a favorite show, having a cup of hot tea while sitting out on your deck. Do something that brings a smile to your face.

Things That Bring a Smile to My Face, by Michelle Market, LPC, CEDS

The color pink
Waterfalls
The ocean
My morning cup of coffee
Apple-picking
Time to myself
Creating a collage
Inspirational quotes
My spirituality
Being slow and present
A heavy rainstorm
A new notebook
A brand-new calendar
Driving in the country
A bouquet of flowers
Petting my dog
Watching a movie in the middle of the day
Sunflowers
Simplicity
Writing
An afternoon nap

Dark chocolate
Sunsets
Water
Mountains
Creeks
The Beach
Sand
Bubble baths
Sunrises
Lavender
Calligraphy pens
Puppies
Kittens
Babies
Fire (sound, smell, sight, and warmth)
Hot cocoa
Making s'mores
A good book
Fresh sheets
Beautiful pictures
Silence

Warm towels
Music
Laughter
Comics
Puzzles
Getting up early
A brisk walk
Planning a trip
Berry-picking
Summer fruit
Picnics
An ice-cream cone
Flying a kite
An outdoor concert
Reading a children's book
Christmas carols
Cutting down a Christmas tree
My favorite candle
My warm robe
My special blanket
Slippers

Create your own list of things that make you smile. Take note to add things that utilize your five senses (sight, sound, smell, taste, and touch). Things that bring a smile to my face . . .

What can I do to take care of myself?

Daily?

_____

_____

_____

Weekly?

_____

_____

_____

Monthly?

_____

_____

_____

Personal Bill of Rights

Part of the journey of having a healthy relationship with food is recognizing the importance of self-care and standing up for your needs. Somewhere along the way you learned to use food as a substitute for those needs. Now it is time to take back the power food has had over you.

A personal bill of rights is a statement of intentions highlighting things that you deserve and things that you have a right to. It is a vital step to taking charge of your self-esteem and practicing self-care.

Sample Personal Bill of Rights

I have the right to be happy.
I have the right to be treated with respect.
I have the right to make mistakes.
I have the right to take care of myself.
I have the right to stand up for my needs.
I have the right to ask for what I need.
I have the right to say no.

Create your own personal bill of rights.

What things are important to you?

       I have the right to_____

       I have the right to_____

       I have the right to_____

       I have the right to_____

       I have the right to_____

       I have the right to_____

       I have the right to_____

Chapter 5 Summary
Self-Care 101

Sleep, good nutrition, and exercise are at the core of self-care. However, that's not where self-care ends! Self-care also entails nurturing yourself emotionally, physically and spiritually. In order to accomplish this, it is vital to carve out time for yourself to allow for rejuvenation.

Self-Care Needs

Physical
- o   Sleep
- o   Moving your body
- o   Nourishing your body at regular intervals throughout the day
- o   Taking time off of work when needed
- o   Taking time to breathe and slow down

Emotional
- o   Saying affirmations
- o   Journaling
- o   Reducing stress in your life
- o   Saying no
- o   Spending time with individuals who you enjoy being around

Spiritual
- o   Taking time for quiet reflection each day (i.e. prayer, meditation)
- o   Reading inspirational writings
- o   Spending time in nature and appreciating your surroundings
- o   Knowing what is meaningful in your life
- o   Knowing what your values and passions are in life

Self-Reflection
One of the ways I am changing is . . .

Healing Practice
Commit to doing more of what you do well. What brings you pleasure? (i.e. volunteering, gardening, exercising, taking a class with a friend) Begin making time in your schedule to implement your self-care plan. Start with just ten minutes per day.

Chapter 6
Creating Pause

Between stimulus and response there is a space.
In that space is our power to choose our response.
In our response lies our growth and our freedom.
—Viktor E. Frankl, MD, Psychiatrist, and Holocaust Survivor

"Live slow." I have always been very curious about this statement. When I am feeling frenzied or feel as if I am juggling many different balls in the air, I often go back to this statement to re-center. Living slowly is very counter to our culture, whether you live in a metropolitan city or in suburbia, the idea of slowing down tends to be one that we resist. Yet it is a vital ingredient to the healing journey. By slowing down and creating pause, you are creating an opportunity to connect with your body and to connect with your feelings. In addition, we are also creating mindfulness in our life. Oftentimes, we are unaware of how fast we are moving through our day, or even moving through our lives.

We see this fast pace in eating practices. When was the last time you sat down and savored what you were eating without any distractions? When was the last time that you really tasted your food and noticed taste, texture, and aroma? When was the last time that you were eating something and you noticed the food no longer tasted as good as the first bite? By creating pause, you are inviting yourself to slow down and check in with your body. How are you feeling? What sensations are you noticing in your body?

When was the last time you sat in silence for any extended period of time? Meditation not only is a healthy coping skill to handle stress, but it is also a tool to help us tune in with ourselves. Quieting our mind results in becoming more centered. When we have slowness in our day we develop greater awareness of what is going on in our mind, body, and with our emotions.

Imagine uninterrupted time during your day to focus on your breathing and slowing down. When you allow your mind to quiet down, how do you feel? Is it uncomfortable? Why might you avoid slowing down? These are questions to consider as you begin to implement the practice of meditation.

It is possible to slow down, although it often needs to be intentional and, initially, rehearsed. Picture the first time you learned to ride a bike. You did not do it perfectly the first time. You fell, bumped into things—you started slowly. Learning the art of meditation and quieting your mind can sometimes feel like the same process.

Steps to incorporate meditation into your day:

- Choose a time in the day that is most conducive to your meditation practice (all you need is five minutes). Initially, it is helpful to set a timer (start at five minutes).
- Find a space where you can sit comfortably. Sit up tall with your legs uncrossed. Have your hands open and palms up. Close your eyes.
- Find a word to focus on that will elicit a calm response. For example, *peace, acceptance, slow,* or *breathe.*
- When other thoughts enter your mind, picture them as clouds floating through the sky and then focus back on the calming word that you had chosen (refer to this as your mantra).
- Take notice of taking slow, intentional, deep breaths: inhaling through the nose and exhaling through the mouth.

I recently participated in an eight-week meditation class. The class met for ninety minutes for eight consecutive weeks. The first week, the class was full. Everyone was sharing and talking about their desire to have a meditative practice. As the weeks went on, the class size shrunk, but then began to grow again. The instructor pointed out to us to take notice of what it took to get us to the class each week. We were reminded that it is okay if we have not been able to create a formal practice, that just focusing on your breath and taking deep breaths each day was enough to create a shift. This was very reassuring because I, like some of the other students, found myself struggling to get to class. I made it each time and compassionately forced myself to spend some time with my mind each week. Week 7 was the most difficult class for me to get to. I literally had a fifteen-minute debate with myself on whether or not to go. The argument went something like this:

Side of me that wanted to skip class: *You have so much to do, just think of what you can do with those two free hours. You can fold laundry, do the dishes, and straighten up around the house. You would feel like you are on top of things.*

Side of me that felt I should go to class: *If you skip, you will miss out on the time to be quiet with yourself.*

Side of me that wanted to skip class: *Well, I did take a yoga class yesterday. Plus, I haven't missed a class yet, so missing one won't be a big deal.*

Side of me that felt I should go to class: *You will not feel the same relief and calm if you stay home. If anything, you will feel more stirred up.*

Side of me that wanted to skip class: *But I haven't done a good job of implementing a meditation routine outside of the weekly practice.*

Side of me that felt I should go to class: *That is even more of a reason to go and to have the structured practice. But remember, during the weeks that you have been taking the class, you have had more patience with the children, you have been more deliberate in slowing down, and you have been breathing more deeply.*

Side of me that wanted to skip class: *But you will never get your things done.*

Side of me that felt I should go to class: *That is okay; you did as much as you can do. Plus, you will feel so much better after you go to the class.*

So I got in my car and started to drive. But I had one more check-in about wanting to skip.

Side of me that wanted to skip class: *You are still so close to your house, you can turn around now and just go back and you will still have a chunk of time to work on things in the house. At this point, you are going to be at least fifteen minutes late.*

Side of me that felt I should go to class: *Just keep driving you won't regret having gone once you get there and get centered.*

I did make it to class, and I was fifteen minutes late. In order to get to class, I drive on some back-country roads. I used the time to get to class to focus on my breathing. The class was held during the fall, my favorite time of the year. As I was driving, I paid special attention to noticing the beautiful trees and the vibrant colors of the leaves. I noticed the horses grazing. I noticed the beautiful lake that I drove by. Had I not had this battle within, I may not have been as appreciative of the drive over, which for the last couple of weeks I had taken for granted. When we begin something new, we do have this resistance and challenge of showing up. When I first began the meditation class, I was really excited and enthusiastic. I also thought it was going to come very easily. What I recognized is that it took planning, patience, and perseverance. All the qualities that are necessary in the healing journey. I still haven't begun a formal practice of meditation, but I am aware of my breathing. I take time to pause and to stop during my day. I take time to check in and to notice what is going on in my body.

It was easier for me to create an informal practice of just focusing on my breath each day at some point of the day. I recognize that it is difficult to create a formal practice of sitting each day. You may find using an informal practice to be a good jumping-off point.

Though there are many different ways to meditate, here are five types of meditations that may be easier to incorporate into your day:

Candle Meditation: Light a candle and place your focus on the flicker of the flame. When your mind begins to drift, re-center your focus back on the candle.

Walking Meditation: Find a path to walk (preferably a scenic route). Take notice of slowing down your steps one foot in front of the other. Take notice of slowing your breathing. Take notice of the scenery, the flowers, the trees, and the grass as you connect with nature.

Cleaning Meditation: Turn any chore into a mini-escape. Take focus on the rhythmic nature of the chore. For example, if you are washing dishes, notice the sound of the water, take notice of the soap bubbles, and take notice of your breathing. Use your calming word to re-center.

Car Meditation: While driving to work or running your errands, turn off the music and drive in silence. Make a conscious decision to practice deep breathing.

Breathing Meditation: A simple way to incorporate calm into the day is committing to taking three deep breaths at different times throughout the day. You can use different transitions as a reminder to breathe, such as before meals, before checking e-mail, before starting the day. You will be amazed at the calming effect that just changing the way you breathe will have.

To sit without any judgment and to invite slowness is a gift of compassion to ourselves. Be patient in the process and start slowly. Begin to look forward to this pause within your day. Make the commitment to incorporate this self-care tool on a daily basis.

"I commit to five minutes of quiet each day."

As you begin this practice on an ongoing basis, you will start to look forward to this time of the day. Meditation provides a bridge to create peace within ourselves. Meditation is a compassionate, nonjudgmental practice to be with yourself each day.

Chapter 6 Summary
Creating Pause

Slowing down is a vital ingredient to the healing journey. By slowing down and creating pause, you are creating an opportunity to connect with your body and to connect with your feelings. When all else fails, just focus on your breath. Notice the inhalation and exhalation of your breath. As thoughts start to enter your mind, allow them to pass on by.

Meditation is a compassionate, nonjudgmental practice to be with yourself each day.

Candle Meditation: Light a candle and place your focus on the flicker of the flame. When your mind begins to drift, re-center your focus back on the candle.

Car Meditation: While driving to work or running your errands, turn off the music and drive in silence. Make a conscious decision to practice deep breathing.

Breathing Meditation: A simple way to incorporate calm into the day is committing to taking three deep breaths at different times throughout the day. You can use different transitions as a reminder to breathe, such as before meals, before checking e-mail, before starting the day. You will be amazed at the calming effect that just changing the way you breathe will have.

Self-Reflection
What are my fears about slowing down and pausing? What stops me from taking the time to stop?

Healing Practice
Practice introducing pause into your day. Start with focusing on your breath.

Chapter 7
Eating Mindfully

How many times have you caught yourself finishing a bag of chips without noticing the taste? When we are eating mindlessly, we are eating without awareness of the present moment. So when you have finished something quickly or without tasting it, I encourage you to reflect on what just happened. Ask yourself, *Why did I just eat that? And what was going on for me at that very moment?* Be curious, but do not judge. Question, but do not shame. Making the connection to being in the present and being mindful is a gradual process. As you start to ground yourself in the art of being mindful and being present, think back to the last chapter, in which I describe quieting your mind. Make that a mantra, to invite you to take a step back. To create a pause instead of reacting. Many times when we emotionally overeat, we are on autopilot. So as you incorporate the practice of pausing, begin to take notice at mealtimes.

The definition of being mindful is being aware of the present moment. The art of mindfulness can be very therapeutic when you allow it to spill into other areas of your life (mentally, physically, and emotionally). When you quiet your mind and check in with how you are feeling, you are practicing the art of mindfulness. Allow yourself to be in the present moment without judgment. Listen to your body. Slow down.

What is mindfulness with respect to eating? It is being aware of what you are putting in your mouth. How many times have you sat down to a meal or a snack and realized that you have not tasted what you had eaten? Why does that happen? The answer: Because we are a society of multi-taskers. So often, you might be eating while watching TV, or while checking e-mail, or while driving from one activity to the next. When we are practicing eating mindfully, we are purposefully paying attention to what we are doing. This is impossible to do when you are multitasking while eating.

The Center for Mindful Eating Defines Mindful Eating As:

- o Allowing yourself to become aware of the positive and nurturing opportunities that are available through food preparation and consumption by respecting your own inner wisdom.
- o Choosing to eat food that is both pleasing to you and nourishing to your body by using all your senses to explore, savor, and taste.
- o Acknowledging responses to food (likes, neutral, or dislikes) without judgment.
- o Learning to be aware of physical hunger and satiety cues to guide your decision to begin eating and to stop eating. (Source: www.tcme.org)

Eating mindfully is being in the present moment with the foods you are consuming. Whether it is breakfast, lunch, dinner, or a snack, eating mindfully is eating without distractions and paying attention to the texture and taste of the food you are consuming. So often we are on autopilot when it comes to eating. We don't catch ourselves putting things in our mouth until after the fact.

What stops you from slowing down and being intentional in your relationship with food?

_____

_____

_____

In what ways are you already incorporating mindfulness in your food relationship?

_____

_____

_____

Mindful Eating Practice:

Allot yourself fifteen minutes of uninterrupted time for this exercise. Supplies needed: two pieces of gourmet chocolate of your choosing.

Chocolate #1: Go ahead and eat the piece of chocolate as you ordinarily would.

Chocolate #2: Place the chocolate in your mouth and allow it to melt. Notice the texture and taste. Is the chocolate smooth? Is it bitter or sweet? Notice how it melts in your mouth. Don't rush the experience; instead, focus on the present situation.

What differences did you notice between the experiences of eating the two chocolates? How might you be more focused in the present with the foods you consume on a daily basis?

_____

_____

_____

Eating mindfully is not as simple as it sounds. What gets in the way may simply be the eating rituals we have established and have yet to break. In Brian Wansink's book *Mindless Eating*, he explores the many traps that we fall into that result in eating more than we planned to. Wansink addresses the idea of "eating scripts." Eating scripts are the rituals that we have created around food. For example, an eating script for Don was that immediately after dinner, he would look for something sweet to eat. Even if he was full from dinner, he never gave it a second thought. It had become his eating script; it was what he would do after dinner.

Mindless Eating Traps:

- A friend suggests getting dessert and you go ahead and agree even though you are feeling full.
- Your spouse reaches for a second slice of pizza and you decide to do the same, even though you were not fond of how the first piece tasted.
- You order the largest tub of popcorn at the movies and eat it during the entire movie.
- Your boss brings donuts to the staff meeting and the tray is sitting right in front of you.

When you eat mindlessly, your eating cues can include the sight of food, the smell of food, the sight of someone else eating, or boredom. Creating awareness gives you the tools to break the cycle.

Mindless Eating Practice:

Take the Mindless Eating Challenge. For the next twenty-four hours, create a log of all the times that you find yourself eating mindlessly.

_____
_____
_____
_____
_____
_____
_____
_____
_____
_____
_____
_____
_____
_____

The following four steps outline a plan to turn mindless eating into eating mindfully.

Step 1: <u>Awareness</u> is being in the here and now with food. It is taking notice of when you are eating. Keep track of all the times you catch yourself putting something in your mouth. Have you ever licked the spoon after making a cake? Finished the French fries your child left on their plate? Found yourself nibbling as you were preparing dinner? Finished a bag of chips while watching your favorite sitcom? These are all examples of mindless eating.

Step 2: Check in with your <u>hunger cues</u>. Say out loud to yourself, "Am I really hungry?" Rate your hunger on a scale of 1–10 (1: ravenous, 10: stuffed). If you rate yourself a 6 or higher, move to step three. *Refer back to Chapter 3 for the Hunger Scale.*

Step 3: Identify the <u>emotion</u>. Check in with how you are feeling. Ask yourself, "Why am I eating?" Are you eating because you are bored, tired, thirsty, sad, etc.? Are you turning to food to cope with uncomfortable emotions?

Step 4: Change the <u>behavior</u>. Do an activity that is not conducive to eating. You might try a craft or activity that uses both hands, such as organizing a cupboard, knitting, etc.

Instead of satisfying the emotion through food, utilize a non-food coping skill. Some non-food coping skills include:

- o Walk away from the kitchen or vending machine
- o Call a friend
- o Drink a glass of water
- o Take a nap

Mindful Eating Practices:

- o Keep eating contained. Only eat in the kitchen. Do not bring food into the bedroom or den.
- o Sit down when eating.
- o Eat without distraction. Turn off the television.
- o Enjoy the experience of eating. Notice the texture, the presentation, and the taste of what you are eating.
- o Slow down the speed at which you eat.

What is it that I want when I am eating, when truly it is not food that I desire?

_____

_____

_____

If I start eating when I am not hungry, how do I know when to stop?

_____

_____

_____

Often, when you struggle with binge eating and emotional eating, there is a disconnect between listening to what your body needs and how you are fueling your body. One of the most critical steps in creating a healthy relationship with food that is intuitive and nurturing is to practice creating attunement. Attunement is a spiritual practice of being aware of our inner self (thoughts, feelings, physiology) as well as our external world (culture, family, external triggers). It is having calm within even when there is chaos existing outside of ourselves.

Chapter 7 Summary
Eating Mindfully

What is mindfulness with respect to eating? It is being aware of what you are putting in your mouth. It is noticing taste, texture, and presentation of the food you are consuming. How many times have you sat down to a meal or a snack and realized that you have not tasted what you had eaten? When we are practicing eating mindfully, we are purposefully paying attention to what we are doing.

Four steps to turn mindless eating into eating mindfully:

Step 1: <u>Awareness:</u> taking notice of when you are eating.
Step 2: Check in with your <u>hunger cues</u>. Say out loud to yourself, "Am I really hungry?" Rate your hunger on a scale of 1–10 (1: ravenous, 10: stuffed).
Step 3: Identify the <u>emotion</u>. Check in with how you are feeling. Ask yourself, "Why am I eating?"
Step 4: Change the <u>behavior</u>. Do an activity that is not conducive to eating.

Self-Reflection
In what ways do I practice being in the present moment when I am eating?

Healing Practice
Practicing eating mindfully at three different meals this week. Eat without distractions. Eat sitting down.

Part Three
Making Peace
with Yourself

Notes:

Chapter 8
Understanding Self-Esteem

Self-esteem: Self-esteem is the ability to value one's self and to treat one's self with dignity, love, and respect.
—*Virginia Satir*

Self-esteem is confidence in oneself. It is viewing yourself in a kind and loving manner. Our self-esteem impacts the way we think, how we feel, and what actions we take. There are two main sources of self-esteem. These are internal sources and external sources. Internal sources of self-esteem include self-like, self-worth, and taking care of yourself emotionally and physically. External sources of self-esteem include looking for the approval of others and a focus on how others define you.

Those with a healthy self-esteem look internally for validation and approval. In essence, you are acting as your strongest cheerleader and believer. When you are validating yourself internally, you are not focused on looking to others to help you feel better about yourself. People with a faulty self-esteem focus on external resources as an indicator for how they feel about themselves. If you have a faulty self-esteem, you look to others to compliment you on your appearance or on your accomplishments. Basing your self-esteem externally gives you a false sense of validation. For every compliment you receive, you feel good. However, when you don't receive positive feedback, or if you are given negative feedback, you feel worse about yourself. When your self-esteem is internally rooted, your image of yourself stays consistent and does not rise or fall based on what others say about you in the course of the day. Your internal validation is a constant.

Internal Sources of Self-Esteem:	*External Sources of Self-Esteem:*
o Feeling a sense of accomplishment	o A focus on how others define you
o Self-like and self-worth	o Approval addiction (always looking for the approval of others)
o Having a sense of self-control	o Positive accolades from others
o Experiencing peace and serenity	
o Happiness	
o Enjoying spending time with yourself	
o Taking care of your needs	

Where are you currently deriving your self-esteem from? Is it externally or internally rooted?

_____

_____

_____

In order to create a strong sense of self, there are certain contributors that accentuate this, I will refer to these as pillars. The pillars of self-esteem that create a strong sense of self include the following:

o Patience with self
o Self-respect
o Self-awareness
o Self-acceptance
o Self-understanding
o Standing up for your needs
o Practicing self-care
o Self-confidence
o Self-love
o Self-forgiveness

For me, self-esteem is practicing self-care; accepting myself instead of comparing myself to others or criticizing myself and my dreams; being patient with myself and accepting that my mistakes are okay and do not define me; liking myself and viewing myself as worthwhile; and feeling confident to make decisions, expand my comfort zone, and share my vulnerabilities.
—One person's perspective

Create your own definition of self-esteem:

_____

_____

_____

How Is Your Self-Esteem?

Rate your current level of self-esteem on a scale of 1–10 (10 being "I feel great about myself" and 1 being "I feel awful about myself"). Why did you assign the rating that you did?

_____

_____

_____

How do you believe your feelings about yourself have impacted your relationship with food?

_____

_____

_____

Which statements currently hold true for you? Mark all those that apply.

- ❑ I am able to accomplish things.
- ❑ I am likable.
- ❑ I like myself.
- ❑ I am able to ask for what I need/want.
- ❑ I am deserving of respect from others.
- ❑ I am confident I will achieve my goals.
- ❑ I am worthwhile.
- ❑ I am always comfortable saying what I mean.

Of the above statements, which one would you like to work toward implementing?

_____

_____

_____

The tragedy is that so many people look for self-confidence and self-respect everywhere except within themselves, and so they fail in their search.
—Dr. Nathaniel Branden

How you view yourself will impact your success. Do you feel that you are a victim of your environment or helpless in the presence of food? One of the first steps in conquering binge eating is to begin to believe in yourself and to value yourself. You are learning to identify your needs and beginning to want what is best for you. Chances are you have been out of touch with your needs. Try this experiment to strengthen your ability to identify your needs. Program your phone to chime three times per day. When the chime goes off, take a moment to look within and ask yourself what you need in that moment. Are you hungry and need to have a snack? Are you thirsty and need a drink of water? Are you cold and need to put on a sweater? Are you tired and need to take a nap? The first step in creating a new relationship with food is learning to care about yourself, even if you are starting with basic needs.

Often it is this negative view of yourself that prevents you from tackling your relationship with food. What you focus on expands. When you focus on the negative, all you will see are the things that are not going well, resulting in a negative view of yourself. If you begin to focus on what is going well in your life, you will begin to notice your successes. Focus on taking charge of what goes into your body. Take back the power that food has had on you. Set realistic expectations for your relationship with food.

Identify three successes from this past week or month related to your relationship with food.

(1) _____

(2) _____

(3) _____

What Are the Sources of Low Self-Esteem?

Low self-esteem often stems from our childhood days. Somewhere along the way, you learned or heard negative messages from others. From these messages, you developed a negative perception of self. Low self-esteem is the internalization of negative messages. This often translates into a negative view of self.

Can you identify with any of these negative messages?

- o   Be nice at all costs.
- o   Children should be seen and not heard.
- o   Keep your expectations low.
- o   Be humble.
- o   Do for others.
- o   Don't rock the boat.
- o   Life is hard.
- o   Don't brag.
- o   Do as I say.

What other negative messages were communicated in the home of your childhood?

_____

_____

_____

What if you had been told these positive messages instead?

- o   You can do anything you put your mind to.
- o   Tell me about your accomplishments.
- o   I am so proud of you.
- o   It is okay to have your own opinion.
- o   There is no need to apologize when you have done nothing wrong.
- o   Be happy.
- o   It is okay to make mistakes.

Core Beliefs

Core beliefs are the assumptions you make about your value and worth in the world. These beliefs directly impact your self-esteem. From this belief system, you create your own set of rules about how you should act in the world. These rules could be ones that were internalized from childhood or have been self-imposed. Core beliefs are often deeply rooted and take time, patience, and persistence to rewrite.

Examples of negative core beliefs:

- o   I am not good enough.
- o   I am not lovable.

- o   Keep the peace at all costs.
- o   My opinion doesn't matter.

Identify your top three negative core beliefs. How are they impacting how you feel about yourself?

_____

_____

_____

Examples of healthy core beliefs:

- o   My needs are important.
- o   I can do things for myself.
- o   I am creating realistic goals.
- o   I am good enough.
- o   What I do is important and hard.
- o   As a human, I have inherent worth.
- o   I matter.
- o   I am a unique person.
- o   I am a person with different views.
- o   My opinion matters.

Challenging Negative Core Beliefs

Take one of the negative core beliefs you identified, and go through the following checklist in order to challenge and rewrite them.

What is the negative core belief? (i.e., I am not good enough.)

_____

_____

Am I looking at the whole picture? (i.e., No, I feel good enough in my personal relationships.)

_____

_____

Create a statement to counter the negative core belief. (i.e., I am enough and it is okay to make mistakes.)

_____

_____

Thirty Techniques to Build Self-Esteem

- o Practice positive self-talk
- o Journal
- o Practice positive affirmations
- o Set goals and follow through with them
- o Talk with a counselor
- o Talk to positive people
- o Take a class on building self-esteem
- o Exercise and eat healthy
- o Make life improvements incrementally
- o Increase self-awareness
- o Practice thought-stopping
- o Do something good for yourself
- o Read self-help books
- o Read inspirational material
- o Volunteer
- o Keep a file of accomplishments and positive letters
- o Eliminate negative people from your life
- o Increase *and* utilize your support network
- o Implement self-care
- o Change your perception of your situation
- o Focus on what is going well in your life
- o Believe in yourself
- o Have a positive outlook
- o Step outside your comfort zone
- o Say no
- o Be a loving friend to yourself
- o Do what you love
- o Focus on the things for which you are grateful
- o Expand your interests
- o Communicate your needs

Chapter 8 Summary
Understanding Self-Esteem

Self-esteem is confidence in oneself. It is viewing yourself in a kind and loving manner. Our self-esteem impacts the way we think, how we feel, and what actions we take.

The pillars of self-esteem that create a strong sense of self include the following:

- Patience with self
- Self-respect
- Self-awareness
- Self-acceptance
- Self-understanding
- Standing up for your needs
- Practicing self-care
- Self-confidence
- Self-love
- Self-forgiveness

Often it is this negative view of yourself that prevents you from tackling your relationship with food. What you focus on expands. When you focus on the negative, all you will see are the things that are not going well, resulting in a negative view of yourself. If you begin to focus on what is going well in your life, you will begin to notice your successes.

Self-Reflection
How is my view of myself getting in the way of tackling my relationship with food?

Healing Practice
Focus on what is going well in your life presently.

Chapter 9
Challenging the Inner Critic

Common Thinking Distortions Associated with Binge Eating

How you view the journey of healing is essential to your success. Adhering to a lifestyle change is truly a lifetime commitment. Cognitive restructuring means changing and challenging your thoughts, especially if they are negative. The first step is recognizing the type of distortion that you have with food and exercise. The four common thinking distortions associated with emotional eating include:

- o All-or-Nothing
- o Shoulds/Musts
- o Filtering
- o Catastrophizing

All-or-Nothing

Dena is notorious for either being on a diet or throwing caution to the wind. When she is on a diet, she is extremely rigid with what she eats and how much she exercises. To Dena, a diet means deprivation. She has her foods categorized as "good foods" and "bad foods." Workouts are extreme. Anything under an hour, in Dena's eyes, is never good enough.

Dena exemplifies all-or-nothing thinking. For the all-or-nothing thinker, there are no shades of gray. This polarized way of thinking leaves no room for moderation. Everything is in extremes. Things are one way and never the other. It is not uncommon to hear Dena declare that she is "on her diet" or "off her diet."

If she deviates from her strict eating and exercise plan and "cheats," she says, "I blew it, I guess I'll start over on Monday," even if it is only Tuesday when her "slip" occurred.

If you relate to all-or-nothing thinking, you are not alone. The majority of individuals struggling with weight have found themselves, at one time or another, thinking in absolutes. The diet mentally sets you up for this type of thinking.

If you are struggling with food one day, instead of throwing caution to the wind, realize that it is okay to backslide, and it is actually a normal process of change. Focus on your successes in weight management. Think in terms of how you made healthy choices for the day, or even for just that meal. Avoid looking at your relationship with food as a diet. Those that have a healthy relationship with food think in terms of healthy lifestyle choices, practicing portion control, and engaging in regular physical exercise.

Shoulds/Musts

Anne was always following rules about what she *should* be eating and how much she *should* be exercising. When you talk to her about her weight-management philosophy, she tells you, "I should only be eating salads and I must never deviate from my diet," a similar philosophy to the all-or-nothing thinker. Her rigidness becomes a vicious cycle as soon as she has difficulty keeping up with her unrealistic expectations. She starts getting down on herself and emotionally beats herself up.

A healthier approach for Anne is to change the messages she tells herself about embracing a healthy lifestyle. Instead of *shoulds* or *musts*, she could tell herself, *I choose to eat healthy*, or *I choose a balanced diet.*

Filtering

David had a difficult time seeing the progress he is making. When someone pays him a compliment, he is quick to discount it. If he is given constructive criticism, he fixates on the negative. When David misses a workout, he focuses on what he has not done versus the significant progress he has made.

Instead of focusing on the negative, take notice of your success. Every positive step counts, no matter how big or small. Focus on what is going well. Did you eat a healthy breakfast? Did you say no to a second helping when you were feeling full?

Catastrophizing

Marie's relationship with food has been a long-standing battle. She has successfully maintained a 100-pound weight loss for approximately three years. Even though she has been consistent with her lifestyle change, she still struggles with her old way of thinking. Marie's greatest fear is that she will gain back all the weight that she has worked hard to lose and keep off. When she finds herself using food as comfort, specifically when she is sad, she tells herself, *Now I am going to gain back all the weight that I worked hard to lose.*

A catastrophizer assumes the worst-case scenario when there is no evidence to support it. In Marie's case, she has had a consistent exercise program for the last three years, she has an excellent support system, and she has taken back the power that food once had over her.

A healthy rebuttal to her negative thinking would be to say, *It is okay and normal to have good days and bad days. If I start to notice that I am going back to my old patterns, then I will take the steps to continue my healthy relationship with food. When I notice that I am eating out of comfort, I will try a non-food activity from my coping-skills list.*

Which thinking distortion do you most relate to? What are some common statements that you say to yourself?

_____

_____

What could you say instead?

_____

_____

_____

Comparison

Comparison is the thief of joy.
—Theodore Roosevelt

We will always find someone who seems to be doing better. Many of us have this default of the grass always being greener on the other side. But the truth is that everyone has their own strengths and weaknesses. Your healing journey is individual; the only person that you should compare yourself to in this journey is you. How is this time different? In what ways are you implementing more self-care? In what ways are you being compassionate with yourself? In what ways are you being curious about patterns and obstacles that you have faced in this journey?

Don't let comparison rob you; instead, choose compassion for yourself. Give yourself all the support that you need in this vulnerable state. As you work through underlying emotions and feelings and you walk through them instead of around them, over them, or under them, you will need to have a healthy dose of compassion on your side.

Self-Talk

Self-talk is the silent conversation that you keep up with yourself for most of the day. This talk can have a direct impact on your thoughts and behaviors. When your self-talk is positive (i.e. "Things will work out" or "I know I can do the job"), you are giving yourself permission to succeed, and chances are you will. When your self-talk is negative (i.e. "I know I am going to have a terrible time" or "I know I am going to fail"), you are giving up on yourself, and chances are that you won't succeed. Often your self-talk reflects the values and behaviors you learned as a child. There is great power in being optimistic about your lifestyle change.

If you are telling yourself fifty negative things in the course of the day, you will need to tell yourself fifty-one positive things to begin to make an impact on your thinking. Don't give power to self-limiting beliefs; instead, refuse to accept them. Realistic self-talk is an example of being positive about the things that you say to yourself. In essence, you are countering unrealistic expectations.

Identify the top five negative thoughts you tell yourself on a regular basis.
(1) _____
(2) _____
(3) _____
(4) _____
(5) _____

As you begin to make this shift in challenging your negative self-talk, begin by being aware of the messages you are telling yourself. Are you on autopilot with the messages you are feeding your mind? The next step is looking at ways to stop the negative thinking. Thought-stopping is a skill that enables you to stop negatively personalizing the messages. For the next week, for every negative thought that enters your mind, tell yourself, *Stop, this is not helpful,* then counter the negative thought with a positive thought. This technique brings the thoughts into your conscious, creating greater opportunity to challenge the thinking. It will also result in greater awareness of how often you are saying negative things to yourself.

Challenging negative thoughts includes refusing to accept it as truth and substituting it for a more realistic and accurate view. Below are some examples of ways to change negative self-talk into positive, affirming messages.

Negative Self-Talk	*Positive Self-Talk*
I am fat.	o I respect my body. o I am doing what is necessary to be healthy. o I am working toward loving and nurturing myself, physically and emotionally. o My size does not define me as a person. o Taking care of myself and feeling confident will make me feel better.
My eating is out of control.	o I am learning to listen to my hunger cues. o I am learning to listen to my feelings. o I am developing new coping skills.
I have no willpower.	o I am listening to my body by eating when I'm hungry and resting when I'm tired.
I have too much weight to lose; it is pointless to try, so why bother?	o Progress, not perfection. If I don't try, the weight will definitely not come off. It requires some effort.

Use the space below to replace your negative self-talk with a positive, realistic statement. The more you become aware of negative thoughts, the greater the chance you will have for challenging them and replacing them with a positive statement.

Negative Self-Talk	*Positive Self-Talk*

Step 1: Create awareness: As Ann began listening to her internal dialogue, she started catching herself when she was engaging in negative self-talk. What Ann didn't realize was how often she was saying negative things to herself. She identified that a trigger for her negative self-talk was when she was feeling lonely. By just being aware, she began feeling more empowered and in control of her thought process.

How often do you catch yourself engaging in negative self-talk? Identify the types of statements you tell yourself.

_____

_____

_____

Step 2: Interrupt the thought: When Ann began hearing negative thoughts, she pictured a bright red stop sign and said to herself, *Stop.* By eliminating a negative thought, you can eliminate emotions and feelings that go along with it.

How might stopping your negative thoughts impact your day-to-day living? Begin to look for ways to stop negative thinking.

_____

_____

_____

Step 3: Challenge the thought: Ann began looking for evidence to support that she is lovable. By playing detective, she realized that she has a supportive family, healthy friendships, and a job that she enjoys. She began finding ways that she was *not* the negative thought.

Begin looking for ways that you can disprove your negative thought. In what ways are you not the thought?

_____

_____

_____

Step 4: Rewrite the thought: Ann began telling herself on a daily basis that she is lovable, and over time she began feeling better about herself. She took that negative thought and replaced it with a positive thought.

Every time you begin to hear your critical voice, replace it with a positive, nurturing statement. Come up with three realistic statements about yourself to challenge your negative thinking.

_____

_____

_____

Thought-Stopping

By eliminating a negative thought, you can eliminate emotions and feelings that go along with it. Thought-stopping is a tool that can be used to facilitate this process. It is very easy to get carried away with negative thinking, simply because these thoughts are automatic.

Thought-stopping techniques

- o Picture a bright red stop sign when you are experiencing negative thoughts and feelings, and tell yourself to stop. Interrupt that thought by saying to yourself, *STOP*.

- o Imagine a file cabinet. When you are inundated with worrisome thoughts or negative thoughts, make a conscious effort to "file away" the thought and tend to it another time.

- o Imagining your negative thoughts as clouds passing in the sky. Allow them to keep moving on.

By practicing thought-stopping, you are giving yourself the opportunity to interrupt negative thinking. You do not have to immediately entertain each thought that enters your mind, especially if it is negative. Start by breaking the cycle of negative thinking. Create a delay, and make a conscious effort not to internalize the thought.

Affirmations

Affirmations are a way to assure that you will start the day positively. They are an important tool in changing your relationship with food. When developing an affirmation, keep the following in mind:

Use the present tense: You do not want to be too focused on the future or stuck in the past. "I choose to eat healthy."

Use only positive words: When you say things such as "I will not" or "I don't," your brain is still hearing the action. For example, if you say "I will not eat chocolate sundaes," what your mind picks up on is *chocolate sundaes.* Instead, try stating, "I make healthy eating choices" or "I eat a balanced diet."

The affirmation should create a strong picture of you, successful in whatever you desire, right now: Do not complicate your affirmations or it will be unrealistic to follow through with them. Instead of, "I exercise every day," state "I exercise on most days."

Keep them short and simple: When they are too wordy, you can get lost in the power of the meaning. You want to be able to recite your affirmations daily. "I am learning to listen to my feelings."

Sample Affirmations

I make healthy food choices, one meal at a time.
I am becoming more physically active.
I pay attention to my hunger cues.
Today, I honor my body.
I love myself and I treat myself with respect.

Try creating three affirmations that you can use on a daily basis. Once you have written them down, say them out loud and post them everywhere you will see them. Surround yourself with these inspirational messages.

(1) _____

(2) _____

(3) _____

Chapter 9 Summary
Challenging the Inner Critic

Common Thinking Distortions Associated with Binge Eating

How you view the journey of healing is essential to your success. Adhering to a lifestyle change is truly a lifetime commitment. Cognitive restructuring means changing and challenging your thoughts, especially if they are negative. The four common thinking distortions associated with binge eating include all-or-nothing, shoulds/musts, filtering, and catastrophizing.

Self-Talk

Self-talk is the silent conversation that you keep up with yourself for most of the day. This talk can have a direct impact on your thoughts and behaviors.

Step 1: Create awareness
Step 2: Interrupt the thought
Step 3: Challenge the thought
Step 4: Rewrite the thought

Thought-stopping techniques

Picture a bright red stop sign when you are experiencing negative thoughts and feelings, and tell yourself to stop. Interrupt that thought by saying to yourself, *STOP.*

Affirmations
- o   Use the present tense
- o   Use only positive words
- o   The affirmation should create a strong picture of you, successful in whatever you desire, right now
- o   Keep them short and simple

Self-Reflection

What keeps you from believing in yourself?

Healing Practice

Identify three affirmations and practice reciting them three times per day over the next week.

Notes:

Chapter 10
Finding Your Voice

Social Support

Research indicates that those with a higher level of support tend to do better in weight-management programs than those individuals without support systems in place. The most helpful type of support is from our peers, especially those who are going through similar struggles with food. Peer support helps with developing self-acceptance, learning new coping skills, and managing stressful situations.

Having support in your healing journey is a critical component. Too often, you might find yourself believing you "should" be able to do this on your own. But that doesn't need to be the case. Just the contrary: We need to have a strong support network in our lives, whether it is family, friends, our faith, or our treatment team. There is no reason that we should do it alone.

It takes a tremendous amount of courage to ask for what you need and to ask for support. If you need practice, start with your therapist or a best friend. Is there something that he or she could do differently to help you build accountability or provide support? Seek out others that are going through the same journey. Move away from isolation, and move toward connection.

A support system is a circle of individuals (personal and professional) that you can turn to for encouragement and support. They have your best interest in mind. They listen to you and provide you with validation of your feelings. Your support system will also challenge you when you need that extra push.

Examples of Supports

1. A counselor
2. A person of your spiritual faith
3. A supportive family member
4. A support group
5. Taking classes on building self-esteem
6. Volunteering
7. A twelve-step group or sponsor

Think of the people in your circle of support. In what ways do they provide you encouragement and support? Do they ask how things are going? Do they applaud and cheer you on? Do they provide you with encouragement when you are feeling down? And most importantly, do you turn to them when you are in need?

Identify at least three forms of support:

_____

_____

_____

Utilizing Your Support System

- Talk about your feelings or thoughts with an understanding person
- Talk to a counselor
- Surround yourself with positive people
- Arrange to be around others when you are not in a good place
- Spend time with people you enjoy
- Spend time with a pet

How do you currently utilize your support system?

_____

_____

_____

What stops you from asking for help and turning to your support system in a time of need? What are you afraid of?

_____

_____

_____

Ways to Ask for Support

As you begin to change your relationship with food, you will notice that you will gain clarity on what your needs are. When you are struggling with your relationship with food, letting others know what you need is paramount.

Wants: What is it that you want? When someone asks you, start to look within; your opinion matters. How might you begin to practice this?

_____

_____

_____

Perhaps in your journey you might desire more support and encouragement. This could take the form of having friends ask you how things are going. Or perhaps you desire your circle of support to commend and acknowledge the steps you have taken and are currently taking in your journey. If food was the focus of your social gatherings with friends or family, make the suggestion of participating in more non-food-related gatherings, such as going for a walk or to the movies. If the topic of conversation centered around discussions of food and diet, ask your circle of support to keep the focus off of food as you are trying to change your relationship with food.

You might tell a friend, "It is really difficult to stick to my eating plan when you insist that we order dessert," or "Right now, while I'm working toward changing my eating, it would be really helpful if I could select the restaurant that we dine at," or "I value our visits together but presently, I find it really challenging to eat out. So for right now, I need to keep our visits focused around non-food activities."

Think of a scenario in which it would be helpful to ask for support. What might you say?

Situation: _____

_____

Response: _____

_____

Learning to Say No

Say no to the things you don't want to do
so that you can say yes to the things you want to.

If you have been a people pleaser and have not been in touch with your own needs, then you may have struggled with saying no to others. To feel empowered in your life to say no, be clear on your priorities, values, and wants. When someone requests something of you, the first thing you can do to give yourself the time and space to think about the request is to tell the person, "Let me check my schedule and get back to you." This buys you some time to go through your own personal checklist to evaluate whether or not you would like to accept the request.

- Is the request reasonable?
- Am I clear of what is being asked of me?
- Is it something that I want to do?
- Is this something I feel obligated to do?

Is the request reasonable?: Is what is being asked of you something you might ask someone else to do? (i.e. a ride to the airport, help babysitting your child)

Am I clear of what is being asked of me?: Ask for more information to clarify what all the facts are. Do you have enough information to make an informed decision? Do you need more information to understand what is being asked of you?

Is it something that I want to do?: When you say yes to a request but are really screaming no on the inside, you end up angry with yourself. Over time, resentment begins to develop and build up, and it distracts you from things you want to do. So start practicing saying no today.

Is this something I feel obligated to do? Are you saying yes because no one else has yet and you don't want to disappoint anyone?

Start with your outer circle and practice saying no to small requests. Begin with the telemarketers and the school committees, and work your way up to those that are more demanding of your time (i.e. friends and family). Remember, don't apologize if it is something that you don't want to do or cannot do. And don't feel that you need to justify why you are saying no. Too often, we get wrapped up in giving lengthy explanations. Or worse, when we feel guilty about saying no, there is a tendency to begin adding things that you can do for the person. (i.e., Your friend asks you to watch her children with little notice, and even though you don't want to, you say yes and then offer to go and pick up the child.) A simple "No, I am not able to" is sufficient.

Identify a situation or area in your life in which you need to start exercising your right to say no.

_____

_____

_____

Chapter 10 Summary
Finding Your Voice

Social Support

Having support in your healing journey is a critical component. A support system is a circle of individuals (personal and professional) that you can turn to for encouragement and support. They have your best interest in mind. They listen to you and provide you with validation of your feelings. Your support system will also challenge you when you need that extra push.

Learning to Say No

To feel empowered in your life to say no, be clear on your priorities, values, and wants. Use this personal checklist to evaluate whether or not you would like to accept the request.

- o   Is the request reasonable?
- o   Am I clear of what is being asked of me?
- o   Is it something that I want to do?
- o   Is this something I feel obligated to do?

Self-Reflection

Who or what do I need to start saying no to?

Healing Practice

Practice this week checking in with yourself as to what you are needing.

Chapter 11
Finding Yourself

Our deepest fear is not that we are inadequate. Our deepest fear is that we are powerful beyond measure. It is our Light, not our Darkness, that most frightens us.- Marianne Williamson

As you continue your healing journey, and your bingeing is no longer serving a purpose, begin to ask yourself, *Who am I?* Healthy self-esteem provides you with the conduit to imagine a life of possibilities. In order to think big, to dream, and most significantly, to follow through, you must keep your commitment to yourself. As your healing journey continues, now is an ideal time to thank the bingeing part of you. Express gratitude for this part of you that was trying to help and protect you.

In what ways has your bingeing served as a protector?

_____

_____

_____

What would you feel you would be giving up by eliminating bingeing?

_____

_____

_____

How has bingeing been an attempt at your own self-care?

_____

_____

_____

What will you do to practice self-care instead?

_____

_____

_____

What do you need to practice to get there?

_____

_____

_____

> *You did then what you knew how to do. When you knew better, you did better.*
> —Maya Angelou

Many people started using food at an early age to self-soothe, to escape, and perhaps survive difficult feelings or circumstances. Food was there. Food was a friend. Food was a parent. Food was quick and easy. Food was an escape. You did the best that you could. Now, as you step back and really look at what was going on back then and how easy it is to slip back into that pattern, take a moment to express gratitude for the bingeing part of you. We do not heal through shame; we heal through our compassion with ourselves.

How might you express gratitude to the bingeing part of you?

_____

_____

_____

> *You gain strength, courage, and confidence by every experience in which you really stop to look fear in the face. You must do the thing which you think you cannot do.* —Eleanor Roosevelt

Who would you be without bingeing?

_____

_____

_____

As you are beginning to take a step back and really come to understand who you are and what needs you have, you might be unclear of what you want or need.

Common needs that we have as humans:

- o Need for connection
- o Need for independence
- o Need for stability
- o Need for support
- o Need for validation
- o Need to be listened to
- o Need to feel heard

What are your needs?

_____

_____

_____

How can you begin to have your needs met? (i.e., Use your voice, Allow yourself to be vulnerable, Accept that you are needs are important and need to be heard, Accept that it is okay and healthy to have needs.)

_____

_____

_____

What judgments do you have about your needs?

_____

_____

_____

What needs are you most afraid of? Take into consideration that sometimes the needs that we are most afraid of are the needs that we need the most.

_____

_____

_____

In what ways can you start to live your life in a positive manner?

_____

_____

_____

What is your vision for the future? Create a collage of images and words that describe where you would like to be in life. Use pictures, images, and sayings to create your future vision.

Create a list of nine things you are. (i.e., I am a loyal friend, I am a hard worker, I am creative.)

I am . . .

I am . . .

I am . . .

I am . . .

I am . . .

I am . . .

I am . . .

I am . . .

I am . . .

Add something that you are not currently, but would like to become. (i.e., I am taking care of my body by moving my body)

_____

_____

_____

What steps will you take to see this goal into fruition? (i.e., Meet with a counselor, Read books on how to take care of my body, Do something daily to treat my body with respect and practice self-care, Go on walks.)

_____

_____

_____

What things/activities in your life bring you joy?

_____

_____

_____

What are the most important things you want out of life, now and in the future?

Physical health _____

Psychological well-being _____

Financial stability _____

Intimate relationships _____

Family _____

Living environment _____

Friends _____

Career _____

Education _____

Personal growth _____

Recreation & leisure _____

Spiritual well-being _____

What do you value? Identify as many things as you can.

_____

_____

_____

_____

_____

_____

Take the values that you identified and chose your top five.

_____

_____

What is your purpose in this world?

_____

_____

What are your top five priorities?

_____

_____

_____

What do you stand for? What are you passionate about?

_____

_____

_____

What is getting in the way of your ability to live the life your desire?

_____

_____

_____

Chapter 11 Summary
Finding Yourself

As you continue your healing journey, and your bingeing is no longer serving a purpose, begin to ask yourself, *Who am I?*

Common needs that we have as humans:
- o Need for connection
- o Need for independence
- o Need for stability
- o Need for support
- o Need for validation
- o Need to be listened to
- o Need to feel heard

Self-Reflection
Who am I without binge eating? What have I been putting off in my life?

Healing Practice
Get reacquainted with you. Take yourself on a date and do something non-food related.

Notes:

Part Four
Making Peace
with Your Body

Notes:

Chapter 12
Honoring Your Body

Acceptance: Accept yourself and where you are right now. As you begin to see yourself in a kinder light, breaking the cycle of self-abuse, you will slowly and steadily make progress toward the change that you desire.

Body Acceptance

Body acceptance and embracing a positive body image are integral parts of having a healthy food relationship. So often, it is easy to fixate on the scale and allow your feelings about your body to embark on a roller-coaster ride of highs and lows based on what the scale is telling you.

One step toward winning the battle against low self-esteem and binge eating is to stop using the scale as an indicator of how you feel about yourself each day. You are a person with good qualities, not a mere number on the scale. Valuing yourself and practicing self-acceptance is the best gift you can give yourself.

The number on the scale *cannot* tell you

You are worthwhile person
You are good enough
What a great person you are
How much you are loved
That you are beautiful inside and out
Your values, interests, and passions
That you are kind
Your self-worth

Don't get hung up on the number on the scale; in fact, throw out the scale. Within the course of a day, your weight can fluctuate. Too often, individuals get hung up on the idea of what the number is. They find they are happy and elated when there is a loss and depressed and frustrated when there is a gain. A healthier measure is to look at how your clothes are fitting. When they are feeling snug, then that is an indicator that you should explore if you are over-consuming calories.

How would you define self-acceptance? What does it look like? What does it feel like? How will you know when you are there? What, for you, is getting in the way of practicing self-acceptance?

_____

_____

_____

Top 10 Ways to Enhance Your Body Image

1. Don't use the scale as an indicator of how you feel about yourself.
2. Create a list of the top ten things that you love about yourself.
3. If looking at fashion magazines results in feeling worse about yourself, cancel your subscriptions.
4. Don't hide away in black clothing; wear colors that are flattering.
5. Don't let your weight hold you back from participating in activities that you enjoy.
6. Find a form of exercise that you enjoy and participate in it on a regular basis.
7. Challenge your negative self-talk with positive, empowering statements. (i.e., "I am stunning inside and out.")
8. Don't wait until you are a certain size to go shopping for yourself; instead, wear clothes that you feel good in.
9. Take care of your body. Treat it in a loving and kind manner.
10. Practice self-acceptance.

Do you find yourself putting things on hold until you reach your fantasy weight? What things are you putting off until you lose weight? How might you incorporate them into your plan?

_____

_____

_____

Some individuals feel paralyzed by fear in their attempts to change their relationship with food. For some it is the fear of failure. (i.e., "If I tell others I am trying to lose weight and don't, I will feel worse about myself.") This creates a cycle of false attempts. For others there is the fear of success. (i.e., "If I lose weight then there will be a lot of focus on me. Success can be lonely.")

Which fear do you identify with?

_____

_____

_____

How is your current weight an obstacle? (i.e., It impacts how I feel about myself as well as other relationships that I am in.)

_____

_____

_____

Write an Apology Note to Your Body.

Dear Body,

I am sorry for punishing you. I am sorry for putting you down. I am sorry for the constant abuse I bestowed upon you. I took you for granted. I am learning to heal and I thank you for all your patience with me. I am learning to take care of you. I am learning to appreciate you. I am learning to treat you with kindness. I realize that I only get one body, and I promise to begin taking care of you. I promise to begin treating you with respect. I am grateful for all you have done for me. I am grateful that each day you give me another chance. Thank you for everything you provide me.

Love,
Amanda

Write your own letter to your body.

Dear Body,

Write a nonjudgmental physical description of yourself.

_____

_____

_____

What parts of your body do you like?

_____

_____

_____

What things about your body cannot be changed?

_____

_____

_____

How does society and the media impact how you feel about your body?

_____

_____

_____

Are you holding on to an unrealistic body image? If so, in what ways?

_____

_____

_____

Identify ten things about your body that you are grateful for:

_____

_____

_____

_____

_____

_____

_____

_____

_____

_____

Who Is Your Authentic Self

Your authentic you is the new beautiful. —Michelle Market, LPC, CEDS

- o She is someone who believes in herself
- o She likes herself
- o She supports herself
- o She honors her needs
- o She knows what is important to her, including her priorities and her values
- o She knows what she likes
- o She speaks kindly to herself
- o She surrounds herself with individuals that love her for her, not because she fits some stereotype of what beauty is
- o She practices patience with herself
- o She has self-respect and practices self-acceptance
- o She knows who she is
- o She has good days and bad days
- o She makes mistakes
- o She isn't perfect

Four Steps to Creating and Cultivating Your Authentic Self

Step 1: Be your own best friend. Treat yourself with the same love and kindness you would a best friend.

Step 2: Build self-esteem. Practice thought stopping to challenge negative thinking.

Step 3: Practice self-care. Nourish your body and nourish your soul.

Step 4: Treat yourself kindly. Say kind things to yourself. Nurture the little child within.

Create your own definition of beautiful:

_____

_____

_____

How can you make sure that you don't feel bad about yourself when you see so-called "perfect" images in magazines or on TV?

_____

_____

_____

What are the qualities you admire about yourself? What things bring you enjoyment? How would a friend describe you?

_____

_____

_____

Make your own commitment to start the change within. Starting today, I will . . (i.e., stop calling myself names, stop comparing myself to unrealistic standards, treat myself with kindness)

_____

_____

_____

*Challenge the following **unrealistic** standards.*

Physically attractive people have it all.

_____

_____

_____

A person's physical appearance defines how they are on the inside.

_____

_____

_____

By controlling how I look, I in turn control how I feel.

_____

_____

_____

What is the purpose of holding on to a negative view of your body?

_____

_____

_____

Practicing Self-Compassion

You must love yourself before you love another. By accepting yourself and fully being what you are, your simple presence can make others happy.
—Anonymous

As you begin to appreciate yourself and start to listen to your needs, it becomes easier to pay attention to the tougher questions. Begin the journey today. Begin to recognize your needs and wants. Begin the process of defining who you are.

How would your life change if you chose to like yourself more? What if you stopped comparing yourself to others? What if you accepted yourself as you are right now? What would your self-talk sound like if you practiced self-acceptance?

_____

_____

_____

_____

_____

_____

What does it mean to be a loving and accepting friend to yourself? How will you know when you are there? What will it look like? What will it feel like?

_____

_____

_____

What gets in the way of practicing self-compassion?

_____

_____

_____

Why is it challenging to be supportive of yourself?

_____

_____

_____

Dear Sandy,

You can do anything you put your mind to. I know things are tough right now, but know that I believe in you, I support you, and I accept you. Things will get a little easier; please be patient with yourself.

Love,
Your Confident Self

Write a letter of encouragement from your confident self. Keep it in a place where you can easily retrieve it when you are having a tough day.

Dear _____,

10 Ways to Love Yourself
Stop criticizing yourself.
Stop taking small problems and turning them into big problems.
Be gentle, kind, and patient with yourself.
Stop listening to negative thoughts.
Praise yourself.
Support yourself.
Take care of your body.
Listen to your intuition.
Believe in yourself.
Love yourself now.

Why are you so hard on yourself? What is it going to take to practice self-acceptance?

_____

_____

_____

_____

_____

_____

_____

_____

_____

_____

_____

_____

_____

_____

_____

_____

_____

_____

Treat yourself the way you would a cherished friend. You forgive her faults.
You tolerate her flaws and mistakes. You cut her lots of slack and you accept her just the
way she is, not how you would like her to be.
Extend that same kindness, gentleness and understanding to yourself this week.
—Life Lessons for Women by Stephanie Marston

Chapter 12 Summary
Honoring Your Body

Body Acceptance

One step toward winning the battle against low self-esteem and binge eating is to stop using the scale as an indicator of how you feel about yourself each day.

The number on the scale *cannot* tell you

- You are worthwhile person
- You are good enough
- What a great person you how
- How much you are loved
- That you are beautiful inside and out
- Your values, interests, and passions
- That you are kind
- Your self-worth

Self-Reflection

What ways are you treating yourself with loving kindness?

Healing Practice

If you have a scale in your home, throw it out.

Notes:

Chapter 13
Moving Your Body

Physical activity is the most important predictor of a healthy lifestyle. Physical fitness has significant psychological benefits to include improved body image and psychological well-being. However, many struggle with how they have viewed exercise in the past. I invite you to begin to look differently at physical activity, create a paradigm shift. Begin to replace the shoulds and the have to's with a desire for connecting in your body, and a desire for moving your body.

Binge eating is about disconnection and recovery and healing is about connecting. Mindful movement is finding joy in connecting with your body. What activities did you enjoy as a child? Did you love to dance? Did you love to ride your bike? Did you like to go on hikes? Or perhaps you had a different experience as a child and did not play as a child. Allow this to be a time for experimentation to find out ways you enjoy to move your body. The intention is to begin to move your body more and most importantly connect with your body. This might begin by beginning to connect with your breathing and gentle stretching.

Barriers to Exercise: Myths Dispelled

I don't have the time to exercise

Don't allow trying to get all thirty minutes of exercise in at one time to serve as a barrier for not getting movement into your day. You will get the same health benefits if you do it all at once or if you break up your exercise into ten minute chunks of time. One is not more advantageous than the other. Invest in a pedometer and start tracking steps per day.

I can't afford a gym membership

You don't need to attend a gym in order to exercise. Sure the gyms want you to believe that their way is the only way. Instead invest in a good pair of walking shoes and walk outside or jump rope. If you have access to stairs, you can get an excellent workout walking or running up stairs. Invest in a pair of hand weights, or a no cost option is always two soup cans.

I don't enjoy exercise, how can I make it more fun?

Try meeting up with a friend for walks or attend a group exercise class. Having that on-going support can be very motivating.

The idea of putting together an exercise program feels overwhelming. I have not exercised in over a year and I have read that you should get 30-60 minutes of exercise daily.

It can feel very overwhelming to put together a program when you have been sedentary for a period of time. There are two techniques you can use when putting together an exercise program (1) shaping and (2) F.I.D. Always check with your physician before beginning an exercise program.

Shaping is gradually easing into an exercise program. For example, you would start out with a 5 minute walk and work up to a 10 minute walk and then a 15 minute walk, and on it goes. Perhaps you would add 5 minutes every week or every few days, depending on how you feel.

F.I.D. is an acronym that stands for frequency, intensity, and duration. To make an impact on your fitness level each week, change one component of the acronym. For example, if you are walking on a treadmill three times per week (frequency) at 3.0 miles per hour (intensity) for 20 minutes (duration). The next week add an additional day so that you are walking 4 times per week (frequency). Or, if walking on a treadmill, add an incline of 3% (intensity). Each week change a different component, depending on how you feel, so that you stay challenged.

Sneak movement into your day

- o   Walk whenever you get the chance.
- o   Park your car at the furthest parking spot.
- o   Take the stairs instead of the elevator.
- o   Make an appointment with yourself to exercise and keep that commitment.

o Just do it. Don't put it off. Tell yourself that you will walk just 5 minutes. Chances are that once you get started you will walk longer.

Moderate physical activities	*Vigorous physical activities*
o Walking briskly (about 3 ½ miles per hour) o Hiking o Gardening/yard work o Dancing o Bicycling (less than 10 miles per hour) o Water aerobics o Weight training (general light workout)	o Running/jogging (5 miles per hour) o Walking very fast (4 ½ miles per hour) o Bicycling (more than 10 miles per hour) o Swimming (freestyle laps) o Aerobics o Heavy yard work o Weight lifting (vigorous effort)

Source: www.choosemyplate.gov

Journaling and Physical Activity

An activity journal is a tool that can assist in keeping physical activity a priority. Keep track of your feelings associated with exercise and moving your body. By journaling and reviewing previous entries, you can remind yourself of the positive impact that you experienced through physical movement. It can also serve as a reminder for what things worked when you followed through with moving your body.

Sample journal excerpt

Alarm clock rang at 5:45 am sharp. I immediately hit the snooze button and thought to myself, maybe I'll start tomorrow. The alarm rang a 2nd time and I forced myself to get up and go downstairs. Thankfully, I had laid out my clothes the night before. I went for a 20 minute walk and that exercise made all the difference in the world. After coming in for my walk, I spent a few minutes doing gentle stretching. I noticed that I had more energy and I was more patient with my children. I did it!!! I recognize that it will take time to get back in shape. I will focus on what I can do today to make healthy choices.

Activity Journal:

_____

_____

_____

_____

_____

_____

_____

_____

_____

_____

_____

_____

_____

_____

_____

_____

_____

_____

_____

_____

_____

_____

Chapter 13 Summary
Moving your Body

Moving your Body

    Physical activity is the most important predictor of a healthy lifestyle. Physical fitness has significant psychological benefits to include improved body image and psychological well-being.

    F.I.D. is an acronym that stands for frequency, intensity, and duration. To make an impact on your fitness level each week, change one component of the acronym. For example, if you are walking on a treadmill three times per week (frequency) at 3.5 miles per hour (intensity) for 20 minutes (duration). The next week add an additional day so that you are walking 4 times per week (frequency). Or, if walking on a treadmill, add an incline of 3% (intensity). Each week change a different component, depending on how you feel, so that you stay challenged.

Self-Reflection

What are the barriers that get in the way of moving and connecting with your body?

Healing Practice

Try a new food this week. Go to the farmers market or produce section and experiment with a new flavor. Connect with your body by trying out a new way to move your body. Have you put off taking a yoga or Pilates class? Create an intention to move your body a few times this week.

Notes:

Part Five
Tools for Your
Healing Journey

Practices to Heal from Binge Eating

Practice One: Understand how your relationship with food began

- What power do I give to food?
- Am I ready to tackle my relationship with food?

Practice Two: Understand the ways you use food to cope

- When do I turn to food to cope?
- Is it when I am bored, angry, sad, lonely, etc.?

Practice Three: Identify your eating triggers and patterns of eating

- What are my environmental triggers that result in overeating?
- What are my emotional triggers that result in overeating?
- What are my most challenging times of the day with respect to eating?

Practice Four: Create pause

- Do I stop and listen to my body?
- Am I am able to slow down?

Practice Five: Eat mindfully

- In what ways do I practice being in the present moment when I am eating?

Practice Six: Utilize Non-Food Coping Skills

- What coping skills have worked for me in place of using food?

Practice Seven: Enhance self-esteem

- How have my feelings about myself impacted my relationship with food?

Practice Eight: Find your voice

- What or who should I be saying no to?
- Who do I need support from in my journey?

Practice Nine: Honor your body

- o   In what ways do I practice self-acceptance?
- o   In what ways do I express gratitude towards my body?

Practice Ten: Follow a healthy eating plan

- o   Have I abandoned the idea that diets don't work?
- o   Do I eat a variety of foods?
- o   Do I allow myself to eat all types of food in moderation?

Practice Eleven: Engage in a consistent exercise program

- o   Is there a form of movement that I enjoy?
- o   What ways am I active in my body?

Practice Twelve: Create intention

- o   What are my daily healing practices?
- o   How am I nourishing my mind, body, and spirit?

Dissecting the binge

Think back to a recent binge without judgment.

What were your feelings and thoughts right before the binge?
If you were to scan your body from head to toe, what would you have noticed was going on in your body?
What were your feelings right after?
What was the role of food in that moment?
Were your nutritional needs met the day of the binge?
Were you connecting with others?
What was the binge trying to tell you?
Were you grounded in your body?
What set you up to binge?
What was the inner you trying to tell you it needed?
What can you do to self-sooth the next time you feel the urge to binge?

_____
_____
_____
_____
_____
_____
_____
_____
_____
_____
_____
_____
_____
_____
_____
_____
_____
_____

Healing Practices

Be aware and just notice how you are around food

Notice thoughts, feelings, and what you are experiencing in your body

Eat without distractions

Eat without judgment

Sit down while eating

Stop eating when you feel satisfied

Notice taste, texture, and appearance of the foods you are eating

Take time to enjoy what you are eating

Legalize all food; notice what you are hungry for

Stop dieting; start listening to your body

Stop and focus on your breath

Feel your feelings

Take a moment to pause

Stop and focus on what is going well in your life

Express gratitude toward your body

Replace negative thinking with positive, realistic thoughts

Notice what environmental and emotional triggers result in turning to food

Identify your needs

Notice how you feel when you move your body

Move your body to have more energy and stamina to live your life

Institute a regular eating schedule

Your Individualized Healing Journey

<u>Healing Bill of Rights</u>

I have the right to honor my feelings
I have the right to a positive, nurturing internal dialogue
I have the right to listen to my body
I have the right to practice self-care
I have the right to be self-compassionate toward myself

Your personal definition of a healthy food relationship:

_____
_____
_____

Favorite coping skills:
(1) _____
(2) _____
(3) _____
(4) _____
(5) _____

Ways to self-soothe without using bingeing:
(1) _____
(2) _____
(3) _____
(4) _____
(5) _____

What are the emotional triggers that lead you to binge? Identify the emotion and then what you can do instead.
(1) _____
(2) _____
(3) _____
(4) _____
(5) _____

What are the environmental triggers that lead you to binge? Identify the environments that trigger a binge.

(1) _____

(2) _____

(3) _____

(4) _____

(5) _____

Supports (friends, family, favorite books, and websites):

(1) _____

(2) _____

(3) _____

(4) _____

(5) _____

Favorite inspirational quotes:

(1) _____

(2) _____

(3) _____

(4) _____

(5) _____

Things you love and accept about yourself:

(1) _____

(2) _____

(3) _____

(4) _____

(5) _____

Things you are grateful for:

(1) _____

(2) _____

(3) _____

(4) _____

(5) _____

Self-esteem-building tools:

(1) _____

(2) _____

(3) _____

(4) _____

(5) _____

Self-discovery:

I need: _____

I require: _____

I deserve: _____

I value: _____

I want: _____

Emotions that you distract yourself from:

(1) _____

(2) _____

(3) _____

(4) _____

(5) _____

What is stopping me? How am I getting in my own way?

_____

_____

_____

Write a letter of encouragement to yourself.

_____

_____

_____

_____

_____

_____

_____

_____

_____

_____

_____

Healing Journey Monthly Checklist

Vision:

What is going well in my healing journey? Am I doing everything I can to create an improved relationship with _____ (fill in the blank)? What needs my attention?

_____

_____

_____

Direction:

Am I stretching out of my comfort zone? Am I doing something differently? Am I challenging myself?

_____

_____

_____

Self-Care:

Am I maintaining healthy boundaries? Do I schedule time for myself? Do I carve out the time for reflection and slowness? Am I nourishing my body? Am I planning out my meals? Do I take time to prepare for the week? Am I listening to my body? What do I need to say no to, so that I have time to say yes to the things that matter? Am I practicing healthy sleep hygiene? Am I going to bed at the same time and getting up at the same time each day? Am I staying physically active (and with balance)?

_____

_____

_____

Support:

Who do I need to reconnect with? Am I reaching out to others? Am I being honest with my treatment team? Am I practicing skills that I am learning in recovery?

_____

_____

_____

Healing Words

Abundance
Acceptance
Authenticity
Awareness
Balance
Believe
Breath
Cherish
Compassion
Considerate
Coping
Deserve
Determination
Dream
Faith
Forgiveness
Fortitude
Gratitude
Growth
Healing
Honor
Hope
Inspiration
Intention
Joy
Kindness
Laugh
Love
Mindfulness
Nurture
Optimism
Patience
Pause
Peace
Perseverance
Presence
Reflection
Serenity
Understanding

Healing Affirmations

I deserve the time and space to heal
I am discovering who I am
I matter
I am enough
I am important
I cherish the person I am
I am practicing patience with myself
I deserve happiness
I am worthwhile
I deserve respect from others and from myself
I honor my feelings
I deserve a great life
I step outside of my comfort zone
I have the right to take things slow
I have the right to take a break when I need one
I have the right to have some quiet in my day
I have the right to express my feelings
I am inspired
I am peaceful
I enjoy fulfilling my potential
I am good enough
I deserve good things
I believe in myself
I practice self-compassion
I listen to my needs
I accept myself
I am okay just the way I am
I am beginning to heal
I can handle it
I can reach any goal that I set
I think and act with confidence
I am worthy of love
I am capable
I can be myself
I am okay as I am
I can _____
I can be _____
I am learning to _____
I deserve _____

Alternatives to Bingeing

Identify three additional alternatives to the emotions listed below.

When I am anxious, I can practice deep breathing.

_____

_____

_____

When I am lonely, I can reach out to a friend.

_____

_____

_____

When I am tired, I can take a nap.

_____

_____

_____

When I am depressed, I can watch an uplifting movie.

_____

_____

_____

When I am feeling stressed, I can go for a walk.

_____

_____

_____

When I am worried, I can challenge my negative thoughts.

_____

_____

_____

When I am angry, I can express how I am feeling.

_____

_____

_____

The Gifts of Healing During Your Journey

The Gift of Support: Don't put a hold on reaching out to others. Stay active in your therapy, whether individual or group support. Bingeing lends itself to isolation, therefore it is important to surround yourself with others who are supportive of your healing journey.

The Gift of Mindfulness: Emotions are information, not something to fear. Be mindful of your feelings and emotions. Honor them, don't criticize them—they are trying to tell you something.

The Gift of Space in Your Schedule: Pay close attention to having some downtime in your schedule, even if you need to schedule it into your planner. Plan for pockets of space within your week.

The Gift of Saying No to Extraneous Obligations: Say no to the things that you don't feel passionate about, so that you can say yes to the things that you do. Be aware of what might excite you, as well as what might drain you. Choose those things in your schedule that energize you and are in line with your values, as opposed to feeling that you should do everything.

The Gift of Saying Yes to Healing: When you put other things in front of your healing, your healing does not have the chance to blossom. Say yes—to yourself.

The Gift of Spontaneity: Ask yourself what you would have fun doing each day. Stop putting your life on hold and waiting until you lose weight to enjoy yourself.

The Gift of Time with Loved Ones: Be especially mindful of being around others that you can be yourself around. This provides the opportunity to cultivate your authenticity.

The Gift of Quiet: Give yourself silence in your day. Turn off the radio and the TV and just notice the silence. Use this quiet time to check in with how you are feeling.

The Gift of Patience: Bingeing did not develop overnight, and it will not heal overnight, either. Be patient in this journey. Don't give yourself a time line. This is a slow and steady process. Allow yourself to build consistently, one meal at a time.

Frequently Asked Questions

1. Why do you not believe in diets?

When you are on a diet you become consumed with thoughts of food. Common diet thoughts include:

- o   When can I have my next snack?
- o   What shall I eat for dinner?
- o   How many calories do I have left for the day?
- o   I better eat all the cookies, candy, chips, and ice cream in the house, because "starting Monday" I am beginning my diet.

By eliminating the idea of dieting, you are reframing your relationship with food. No longer are there "bad" foods or a sense of deprivation. Practicing conscious eating abandons the deprivation-and-binge cycle that too often accompanies dieting. Remember, diets are external and eating intuitively is about creating attunement. Attunement is listening to your body. Specifically, listening to hunger cues. Ask yourself the essential questions:

(1) Am I hungry right now?
(2) Why am I eating?
(3) What does my body need?

2. How often should I eat?

Institute a regular eating schedule. Going long periods of time without eating is one of the most common triggers for overeating. By establishing a regular eating schedule (breakfast, mid-morning snack, lunch, afternoon snack, dinner, and optional nighttime snack) you allow your body to become a regular guide for hunger and fullness. Hunger is a signal that your body needs fuel. When you eat on a schedule, you avoid the extreme hunger that results from skipping meals or snacks and often triggers overeating. A regular eating schedule helps to provide some structure to your dining habits.

3. What is a balanced diet?

According to Choose My Plate, it is an eating plan filled with a variety of foods. Balanced eating is eating a variety of fruits and vegetables, incorporating whole grains and calcium-rich foods, consuming lean proteins, and monitoring sugar, fat, and oil intake. When you are eating the same thing every day, you will get bored and will be back in "diet" mode. Balanced eating is something you can do for the rest of your life. Remember, this is a lifestyle change, not a fad or quick fix.

4. Any words of advice for someone making the transition to eating mindfully?

Plan, plan, plan! Plan your meals. Have snacks readily available. Don't allow much time to lapse between meals. Have a variety of healthy foods in your pantry. Eat sitting down. Don't eat in the car. Don't eat in front of the TV or in front of the computer screen. Slow down. Enjoy the texture, taste, and presentation of your meals. Bring your eating into the here and now.

5. I hate breakfast, but I keep hearing of the importance of eating breakfast.

Breakfast is an excellent way to jumpstart your day. Research shows that those who eat breakfast daily keep the weight off long-term, compared with those who don't. If you don't like breakfast foods, there are other ways to jumpstart your day. Try:

- A yogurt shake and piece of fruit
- A handful of nuts accompanied with a turkey-and-cheese roll-up
- Last night's leftovers
- A peanut-butter-and-jelly sandwich on whole-wheat bread

6. What are common eating triggers for overeating?

In the twelve-step arena, the acronym H.A.L.T. is a quick way to be cognizant of triggers for relapses. H.A.L.T. stands for "hungry, angry, lonely, and tired."

7. What is the best form of exercise?

The best form of exercise is one that you enjoy and you are committed to. The bottom line is to start moving your body more and to connect to your body.

Some strategies for incorporating more activity into your day include:

- Go for a ten-minute walk first thing in the morning.
- Take the stairs instead of the elevator.
- Park at the farthest parking spot
- Instead of e-mailing your coworker on the third floor, deliver your message in person
- Turn on your favorite CD and dance
- Garden outdoors

8. I find that every afternoon around 3 p.m., I hit the vending machine for a candy-bar fix. What can I do instead?

You are not alone. Many people suffer from the afternoon slump. Instead of reaching for a sugar rush, which will give you a false sense of energy followed by a crash, try:

- Going for a walk around your office building
- Having a sensible snack such as:
    - a piece of fruit and a handful of nuts
    - string cheese and whole-wheat crackers
    - 1 tablespoons of peanut butter with an apple
    - 1 tablespoons of hummus with a whole-wheat pita
- Taking a fifteen-minute power nap

9. What are some strategies for being successful when grocery shopping?

These simple steps will guarantee you a successful grocery trip:

- Never go food shopping on an empty stomach (it will be harder to make healthy choices).
- Shop from a list and stick to it (again, avoid buying something because it "looks good").
- Shop the perimeter of the store (there are hidden traps/triggers in the middle, i.e. candy, high-fat snacks, high-sugar cereals).
- Buy healthy foods.
- Stock up on fresh fruits and vegetables in the produce section.

Food Journal

Time	Type of Meal B/L/D/S (Breakfast, Lunch, Dinner, or Snack)	What did I eat, and how much?	Initial Hunger Level (1–10)	Where was I eating (environment)? Was I doing anything else while I was eating? (i.e. watching TV, standing up)	How am I feeling?	Ending Hunger Level (1–10)

Special Section for Mothers
The Kitchen Trap

Many mothers find themselves the gatekeepers of the food: preparing meals, doling out snacks, cleaning up after meals. These can all serve as hidden-calorie traps. When you are constantly around food, it is important to have a plan as to how you will handle unconscious eating.

A common trap for mothers is the food their children leave on their plate. Over the course of the day, those calories can add up and you can lose track of all that you are putting in your mouth. Keep a food journal of what you are eating. A food journal will create an awareness of what you are consuming. It will also help you think twice before eating the half of a grilled-cheese sandwich left on your daughter's plate.

As a mother, what you are your hidden calorie traps?

_____

_____

_____

Below are some common reasons mothers find they overeat and some strategies to combat those feelings and/or situations. Create awareness as to why you are eating and what it is that you want.

I tend to overeat when I am preparing dinner.

Do you find yourself snacking while you are preparing dinner, and then by the time dinner is ready you are not hungry? Some strategies to combat this eating trigger include:

- o Prepare meals in advance. If you are too hungry at 5:00 to start preparing dinner, have a day of the week that you do your meal-prep work so that all you are doing is putting your meal together, reducing the time spent doing prep work right before dinner.
- o Cook dinner earlier in the day, during non-trigger times. Then all you need to do is reheat your food when it is dinnertime.
- o Have a healthy snack before preparing dinner, such as a slice of whole-wheat toast with a tablespoon of peanut butter and half a glass of skim milk.
- o Chew a piece of gum or suck on a hard candy while preparing dinner.

I find myself overeating when I am tired, looking for a quick energy boost
to get me through my day.

Many mothers do not have the luxury of taking daily naps, sleeping in, and for some, even sleeping through the night. Some ways to combat tiredness include getting some form of exercise each day. Just ten minutes can make all the difference in the world.

Have a time of the day for scheduled downtime. Implement fifteen minutes of quiet time in your house during which your children must be quiet and the television is turned off. It is both good for you and good for them. Use that time to rejuvenate—leaf through a magazine, sit on the couch and close your eyes, practice deep breathing. You owe it to yourself to have some downtime.

As much as I love being around my children,
I find myself bored and eating as a result of that.

There are times when you find yourself going through the motions, reading <u>Green Eggs and Ham</u> for the fiftieth time. As a mother, you are on call 24 hours a day, 7 days a week, with no sick leave or vacation time.

If you have ever traveled on an airplane, you have probably heard the flight attendant gently remind you to put on your own oxygen mask first in an emergency before assisting others. Similarly, in your personal life, if you do not first meet your own needs, it can be quite difficult to have the energy or resources to take care of others. An uncompromising regimen of self-care is, in effect, the daily dose of oxygen you need to store up your physical and mental resources.

But what exactly is self-care? Sleep, good nutrition, and exercise are at the core of self-care. However, that's not where self-care ends! Self-care also entails nurturing yourself mentally and emotionally. In order to accomplish this, it is vital to carve out time for yourself to allow for rejuvenation. One caution: Sometimes, when we think we have to "take care of ourselves," we create rather elaborate plans that just don't get put into play. Rather than thinking on such a large scale, the key is to start small. Even simple pleasures can bring increased joy into your life.

Here are a few ideas to get you thinking about your own self-care plan:

o   Create a mommy time-out. Allow yourself 15 minutes of un-interrupted time. In essence, you are modeling to your children the importance of recharging.
o   Listen to relaxing music at home.
o   Plan fun and/or relaxing activities into your day on a regular basis.

- ○ Focus on daily pleasures (i.e., the change in color of the leaves, a beautiful sunset, watching your children play).
- ○ Schedule a "me date"—block out time just for you on a weekly basis; perhaps this might be best accomplished by trading off with a friend. They watch your children for a block of time, and in return you watch their children. Challenge yourself to only do things for yourself during that time (no running errands, grocery shopping, getting the oil changed in the car!). Luxuriate in a few hours of time just for yourself.
- ○ Schedule physical activity into your day—just 10 minutes can give you a boost.
- ○ Unwind at night with a warm soak in the bathtub.
- ○ Light an aromatherapy candle and practice deep breathing.
- ○ Ask for support.

How can I exercise with small children needing my attention?

This can be very challenging, and yet does not have to serve as a barrier. Take your toddlers for a walk. Just the added weight in the stroller can give you a good workout. Many shopping malls open up early to allow for walkers; take advantage of that.

Turn up the music and dance with your children; they won't even realize it is your planned exercise for the day. Play a game of outdoor tag with your little ones.

As a parent, you are a role model and have the ability to create a powerful message about the importance of exercise. This is especially important for today's children, given the increase in computer use, television watching, and motorized scooters. Our youths need to learn the importance of daily physical fitness. As a whole, our society is becoming more sedentary. Bring back the old games of "Red Rover," "Red light, Green light," and a good old-fashioned game of freeze tag.

Resources

Recommended Websites

www.eatright.org

The official website of the American Dietetic Association. Featuring nutrition tips of the day and up-to-date food and nutrition information.

www.choosemyplate.gov

The website of the U.S. Department of Agriculture's Center for Nutrition Policy and Promotion (CNPP). Educational material on MyPlate features dietary guidelines, tips, and resources. It also includes the ability to create an individualized plan based on your age, gender, and physical activity.

www.tcme.org

The Center for Mindful Eating (TCME) features educational material on eating mindfully. Provides a quarterly newsletter for individuals and families to help adopt the principles of eating mindfully.

www.bedaonline.com
Binge Eating Disorder Association (BEDA) is a community of treatment providers, people with eating disorders, families, educators and activists united to help those with binge eating disorder.

Recommended Reading

Tribole, E. and Resch, E. *Intuitive Eating: A Revolutionary Program That Works.* New York: St. Martin's Griffin, 2003.

Wansink, Brian. *Mindless Eating: Why We Eat More Than We Think.* New York: Bantam Dell, 2006.

Michelle Market, LPC, CEDS

Michelle Market, LPC, CEDS is a Licensed Professional Counselor (LPC) and Certified Eating Disorder Specialist (CEDS). Michelle is dedicated to helping adolescents and adults feel better physically and emotionally through counseling, coaching, and workshops. She has a private practice in Herndon, VA, as well as a virtual practice, and specializes in binge eating, self-esteem, and eating disorders. Her mission is to create and maintain positive change in the lives of her clients.

Michelle began her career in corporate wellness before becoming a Licensed Professional Counselor, Wellness Coach, and speaker. She views the therapeutic and coaching process as a collaborative journey of discovery and growth.

Michelle obtained her Bachelor of Science degree in Human Nutrition and Foods from Virginia Polytechnic Institute and State University in 1995 and a master's degree in Counseling and Development from George Mason University in 2000. A combined background in counseling and nutrition has allowed Michelle to offer a unique wellness approach when working with clients who struggle with their relationship with food.

Michelle speaks to audiences regarding making peace with food, enhancing self-esteem, and implementing self-care. Michelle offers ongoing support groups on binge eating, eating disorders, and self-esteem. Michelle offers phone retreats for healing from binge eating www.michellemarket.com

For more information on retreats and additional resources for binge eating www.healingforbingeeating.com

Made in the USA
Middletown, DE
27 March 2021